Repair Your Credit Like the Pros

How credit attorneys and certified consultants legally delete bad credit and restore your good name

Carolyn Warren

Bestselling author of *Mortgage Rip-Offs and Money Savers*

Disclaimer

Neither the author nor the publisher assumes any responsibility for interpreting or implementing this book. Nor is this to be considered legal advice. Consult your attorney or CPA for legal advice.

Table of Contents

Chapter 1 Yes, Credit Repair Works 1

Chapter 2 How to Properly Dispute Negative Accounts 11

Chapter 3 How Fast (and How Much) Will Your Credit Score Improve? 27

Chapter 4 What the Credit Bureaus Don't Want You to Know 31

Chapter 5 What Credit Counseling Groups Don't Want You to Know 37

Chapter 6 What the Lawyers Don't Want You to Know 41

Chapter 7 What Credit Repair Companies Don't Want You to Know 43

Chapter 8 What the Federal Trade Commission Doesn't Want You to Know 47

Chapter 9 The Inside Scoop on Credit Scoring 53

Chapter 10 Credit Scoring and the Automobile Industry 59

Chapter 11 How Credit Scores are Calculated 61

Chapter 12 Quickest, Easiest Ways to Raise Your Score 65

Chapter 13 How to Get an Awesome Score of 800+ 69

Chapter 14 Getting Late Payments Deleted Like the Pros 73

Chapter 15 Deleting Collections and Charge-Offs Like the Pros 79

Chapter 16 How to Handle Medical Collections 95

Chapter 17 Deleting Judgments and Liens Like the Pros 101

Chapter 18 Dealing with a Bankruptcy.................................107

Chapter 19 Handling a Foreclosure Like the Pros.................117

Chapter 20 Removing Extra Names and Addresses From Your Report....121

Chapter 21 Delete Inquiries Like the Pros..........................129

Chapter 22 Build Great Credit and Achieve a High Score.........133

Chapter 23 Is Credit Repair Ethical?................................147

Chapter 24 Conclusion..151

CHAPTER 1

Yes, Credit Repair Works

Are you sick and tired of being rejected and embarrassed because of bad credit? Are you fed up with paying more for credit cards and insurance premium because of your score? Do you want to buy a house and get the best possible rate and terms? Do you want your credit report to reflect a good image of yourself and to honor your good name? Are you frustrated with errors and false information on your credit report?

If your answer is yes to any one of these, then GOOD FOR YOU! Now is the time to take control of your credit, improve your score, and reach your goals.

Here is the story of how one man went from being a renter to owning a nice home with acreage by cleaning up his own credit.

Going From Rejection to Approval in Less Than 90 Days

Mr. Steve McAllister of Iowa gave me permission to use his real name and tell his story.

On November 12, Mr. McAllister had an opportunity to buy a home that he didn't want to pass up. He knew the owner of the house, and she was willing to sell to him at an excellent price. The only problem was that every bank and mortgage lender had turned him down for financing due to his low credit score.

Mr. and Mrs. McAllister were honorable people, not deadbeats. Their bad credit began when he was diagnosed with a rare form of cancer. The doctors rushed him into an aggressive treatment program in an all-out effort to save his life. Understandably, bills piled up during that time when he was too sick to get out of bed. Some of the bills even slid into collections.

Then the day came when Steve received a clean bill of health. He beat the cancer! Now it was time to put his life back in order, including working on his credit. This is when he found my credit improvement system (which is this book, now updated).

The strategy was to get rid of old, derogatory accounts in a manner that is legal and permanent, pay down high balances, and to maintain good credit going forward. He started on November 12th and on January 6th, his credit score had risen by 112 points. This enabled him to get approved for an excellent, low rate FHA loan with only 3.5 percent down payment.

By mid-February, he closed on his loan, and he became a proud and happy home owner. His life was not only back on track, but he was moving forward better than ever!

Is It Legal to Have Derogatory Credit Removed?

First, you need to know that it is absolutely legal to have late payments, collections, and other negative items deleted from your credit report. If it were not legal, there wouldn't be attorneys and law firms specializing in doing this. There wouldn't be bankers and brokers getting their clients' credit cleaned up. There wouldn't be professional credit repair companies still open for business *after being audited by government agencies*. It is legal to repair your credit, and you can do it yourself rather than pay someone else to do it, if you so choose.

Here are the facts that explain why the pros are able to get derogatory ratings removed:

1) The credit bureaus are *not* government agencies and reporting to them is optional.

A common misunderstanding is thinking the credit bureaus are part of the U.S. government. The fact is that Experian, Equifax, and TransUnion are private enterprises. They were not set up by the government, they are not owned by the government, and they are not run by the government. There are laws they have to abide by, but then that is also true for other types of businesses as well.

Think of it this way: Some dudes got the brilliant idea to keep track of everybody's spending and bill paying habits—and what a money-maker that idea that turned out to be! They sell this personal information to create extreme wealth for themselves. TransUnion is owned by one of Chicago's wealthiest families, perhaps second only to Oprah Winfrey. Equifax, now a public company, rakes in $1.5 billion per year (per Wikipedia). Experian is a U.K. company with an office in the United States.

The way the bureaus gather personal information about you and other consumers is to have companies report it to them. Since each credit bureau is privately owned and not a government agency, nobody is required to oblige their request for information. This means that credit card companies, department stores, automobile finance companies, and even mortgage companies do not have to report your payment information to the credit bureaus if they don't choose to.

Furthermore, bankruptcy courts do not provide information to the credit bureaus; all information the bureaus obtain about someone's bankruptcy is through third parties. More about that later in Chapter 18: "Deleting a Bankruptcy."

IMPORTANT POINT Reporting your payment history to one, two, or all of the credit bureaus is 100 percent voluntary. It is not required by law. This applies to both positive and negative credit.

If a mortgage company wants to report your house paying habits to a credit bureau, it can—but it certainly doesn't have to. Your loan file belongs to the mortgage company. They keep track of who pays on the 1st of the month, on the 5th of the month, and who goes late after 30 days. It is their own private information about their own private customer. If they choose to report it, they can; but they can also choose to ignore the bureaus, which is what some of them do.

Personally, I used to work for a mortgage lender that never reported any of their customers' payments, whether on time or late. Why? Because the lender knew that their competitors trolled credit reports for home owners to solicit to refinance, and they didn't want their customers stolen away by another lender.

Another good example is cell phone companies. Most of them do not report your payment history, whether on time or late, to the credit bureaus. The exception is if your bill goes extremely late and into the collection department. Typically, they will report a cell phone account that is in collections.

Additionally, electric companies, cable television, rent management companies, as well as doctors and dentists don't choose to report to the credit bureaus, unless your account goes into collections. So even if you pay these bills on time every month, year after year, you won't get one single positive point on your credit score for it.

Another twist is that some companies report payment history to one credit bureau but not to all. This is why a person's credit scores can vary widely from one bureau to the next. Not all of the credit bureaus will have *all* of your credit information. In reality, none of the credit bureaus have all of your information; they have only the information that has been voluntarily reported to them by the companies that have chosen to do so. This leads right into the next fact.

2) There is no law that says a late payment must be reported.

If it is voluntary to report information to the privately-owned credit bureaus, then in turn, it is voluntary to report negative information, such as a late payment, collection, or charge-off.

IMPORTANT POINT If creditors don't have to report information about their customers, then they can also change information about their customers. Like if they made a mistake. Or if they decide to give grace and ask for the negative information to be removed, or if they decide the customer deserves to have the negative information removed early. And guess what? Companies do this all the time! (How to persuade them to do this is coming up later. Hint: It is not by giving them a sad sob story or explaining all your troubles.)

3) Your payment history is owned by the individual creditor/company, not by the credit bureaus.

Let's say you bought a Ford and used Ford financing. You paid Ford on time every month for two years, and then you got appendicitis and went into the hospital, so that one month, your payment got skipped. Ford has it on record that you were late one month. So now what? Ford can choose to report this information to the credit bureaus or to keep it private. These records belong to Ford, not to anyone else.

Experian, Equifax, and TransUnion do not own your payment history for your Ford automobile. Only the Ford financing company owns those records. Even if Ford chooses to pass on the information to the credit bureaus, they still are the owners of the information.

This makes sense, doesn't it? Think about it: why would the individuals who started the credit bureau own your payment records for Ford? They don't! More about this later, but this is a "light bulb moment" for a lot of folks. If Ford owns the records, Ford also has the legal right to modify or change or delete the records if they so choose. And, there are very good reasons why a company might choose to do so.

If they want to give you grace because of your hospitalization with appendicitis or for any other reason, then they can do that. If you were the daughter of the President and CEO of Ford, don't you think you might get some grace? See what I mean? So yeah, *they can do that.*

Attorneys who specialize in credit repair and other credit professionals write letters that persuade companies to remove the late payments. Later, you will see the actual letters that make those late payments disappear, so you can use them for yourself. To save you time, I will give you these letters in a .doc file so you can simply fill in your own information and edit as appropriate without typing the letters out from scratch.

The Credit Bureaus Have Made a Big, Fat Mess of Our Credit Reports!

If you know 100 people, 26 of them have errors on their credit reports. Makes you wonder if you are one of those 26 people, doesn't it? Can you imagine any other business messing up on one out of four customers and still staying in business? And we're not talking about getting you the wrong pizza topping! We're talking about errors that prevent people from becoming home owners and errors that make people pay a high interest rate for their auto financing. These statistics come from a reputable and recent source: a 370 page report released by the Federal Trade Commission in October 2013. (And it has not improved so far in 2016.)

The silver lining to this colossal mess is that when you dispute negative information—using the language and format the professionals use—you have a credible chance of getting that unwanted information removed from your report.

IMPORTANT POINT If you make one of the common mistakes while trying to dispute derogatory credit, you could inadvertently "cement" that bad credit into stone on your report and make it virtually impossible to remove. Many people have learned this the hard way, and that is why some people think disputing bad credit doesn't work—because they approached it incorrectly. Hint: Attorneys and certified credit consultants *don't* use the online forms provided by the credit bureaus and *neither should you!*

When you know how to repair your credit in a manner that is both legal and credible, you take control. No more being a victim to the system! You hold the power to your own credit score.

Author's Credentials

Working as a partner with what I consider to be the top credit restoration service and foremost credit expert in the United States, I learned insider secrets that are never revealed to the public. The company (named later) does the difficult credit work that law firms and other credit companies are not able to do. After those companies completed as much as they could, the clients came to us to finish the most gnarly work. The owner of the company has over 25 years' experience and is amazing in his ability to negotiate and get the job done. This credit expert was and still is my credit mentor. In addition, I have conducted interviews with other certified credit repair specialists and with employees of ARC, an American credit reporting company.

With over a decade of experience in the mortgage business, working in both retail and wholesale mortgage lending, I have helped my own clients repair their credit and restore their high scores so that they could get a low-cost home loan. In fact, Mr. Steve McAllister, whom you read about earlier, was one of my clients. I helped him get an excellent FHA loan that required only a small down payment. One of my tasks was negotiating with collectors. I worked with collection companies—both local to me and across the United States. I worked with a group of attorneys in Georgia who specialized in collections.

I have been behind closed doors in both large and small collection offices. To enter, I had to go through a secret, unmarked door in the back of the building. What I saw inside was interesting, to say the least, and I tell you more about that in Chapter 7 "What the Credit Repair Companies Don't Want You to Know."

I have conducted credit seminars for mortgage loan officers, teaching them how to help their own home buyers. Interestingly, a few of those loan officers asked to speak with me privately after the seminar. They confided that they, too, needed credit repair for themselves. They were embarrassed about having poor credit personally when they worked in an industry that qualifies people based on credit. By using my system, they were able to restore their good names. One went on to buy a $975,000 Street of Dreams home in Woodinville, WA, and he and his wife invited me to their housewarming party.

Looking Ahead

In the upcoming chapters, you will learn about strategies and tactics used by the certified credit repair specialists. Once you know how they do their work to delete negative items from credit reports, you have the choice of doing it yourself and saving the cost of hiring a professional.

FICO 9, a new algorithm for credit scoring was released in 2014. These changes are important for you to know, because it changes the advice about how to handle some types of derogatory credit.

You'll also discover important information on creating the highest score possible. You will learn little-known facts such as how many credit cards to have for the highest score and why paying off an old late bill can instantly lower your score by 30 to 50 points.

In Chapter 11, "How Your Score is Calculated," you'll learn why your score can drop by 50 to 80 points in one day, even when you haven't changed a single thing about your credit.

A lot of people wonder why their automobile insurance company charges a higher premium if a driver doesn't have top tier credit. They think it's bogus and unfair. The scoop is in Chapter 10.

By reading the Table of Contents, you'll see all the topics that are covered in this book. Please feel free to skip around and read the chapters in whatever order you like.

As a bonus for my readers, I give you the letters for deleting late payments, collections, judgments and liens, old bankruptcies, extra names, incorrect addresses, and false inquiries. You can use these letters without having to type them out yourself. These are templates where you fill in the blanks for your own name, address, account number, etc. You can edit as desired without having to compose them yourself. Instructions for getting these templates are in the chapter called, "Conclusion." My checklist for repairing credit is also there, so you have a handy list for what to do first, second, and so on. By this point, you've read all the insider information and are ready to get to work.

So let's get started!

CHAPTER 2

How to Properly Dispute Negative Accounts

You can have negative items such as late payments, collections, and charge-offs deleted from your credit report by following these four simple, straight-forward steps.

Step One: Order your credit report from each of the three credit bureaus by mail.

To challenge a credit bureau regarding the information posted, you must first order your credit report, because you need to reference and work off of that report. You cannot work off of a credit report you received from your loan officer or from a different website. You must order from the bureaus themselves. This is easy to do, and you are entitled to one free report per year from each of the three bureaus, thanks to a law enacted December 4, 2003 by President Bush.

Using the Online Credit Dispute System is Like Shooting Yourself in the Foot

Even though it's more convenient, you must not order your report on the Internet. Don't make the mistake of doing it the lazy way! Do you think the bureaus set up online disputing for your advantage or for their own? Order by mail, receive by mail, and dispute by mail.

IMPORTANT POINT Online credit disputing is ineffective. It puts serious limitations on your rights, with limited statutes. Most people don't realize that when they proceed with the online system, they have accepted those terms and conditions, because *who actually reads through it all?* By using their website, you waive important consumer rights.

The best credit repair companies work their "magic" through the United States Postal Service.

Look at what credit attorney Chi Chi Wu said in a report called "Automated Injustice":

"The (online) forms only help the bureaus steer your issue into one of their dispute buckets, helping the agency automate your claim. It also means you'll have less of a paper trail to demonstrate negligence later on."

I'll explain.

The Electronic Online System for Correct and Accurate Reporting (E-OSCAR) was created by the big credit bureaus for their own purposes, to speed up the process for themselves and to quickly eliminate as many dispute requests as they can. It was not designed for the best interests of the consumer, so make a note of that.

Each time you submit a dispute online, their E-OSCAR system translates your request into a two or three digit code. Thus, you become nothing more than a number. The code may or may not accurately reflect your situation. There is no humanity involved. There is no common sense involved. You get turned into one of four or five reason codes. Sometimes, there might not even be an accurate code for your situation; and in that case, you get put into a so-called similar code, which could automatically shoot your efforts right out of consideration.

What's more, if your dispute gets coded wrong, the likelihood of you being able to get it changed is extremely low. When you try to change it, they think you're on a fishing expedition, trying to scam the system, which results in an automatic rejection letter. (It's no wonder why some people think credit repair doesn't work! They go about it like an amateur, not like the pros.) But wait, there's more!

When you file online, you don't have the ability to attach documentation that proves your case. This leaves you vulnerable to E-OSCAR labeling your dispute as "frivolous and irrelevant." That is the last thing you want to happen, because it prejudices the system against you.

Furthermore, if you don't use the good old-fashioned USPS mail, you waive your legal right to receive written results of the credit bureau's investigation. The bureaus are not required by law to send you any written results of investigating your dispute when you file electronically. Therefore, you give up a big advantage, and you can't afford to do that.

Online, you also waive your right to sue the credit bureau for mishandling your credit. You don't want to give up that leverage (or the threat of using that leverage).

Using E-OSCAR does not save you time if it doesn't get you the results you want. The next time you hear a speaker or see an article that says to use the online system at the credit bureaus' websites, roll your eyes and ignore them, because they are not true experts on credit repair. Similarly, if you hear a story about how it worked for someone, it doesn't mean you should take the risk yourself. It's better to stack the odds in your favor, not to risk it because someone else got lucky.

IMPORTANT POINT Never order your credit report from a website advertising free credit scores, because you will not have the correct report for communicating with the bureaus. Moreover, the scores you receive are not necessarily accurate. Many scores from third party websites give out scores that are artificially high by 20 to 70 points, which sets you up for disappointment later. *They are not using the same scores used by the mortgage industry.*

There are multiple websites that look official, but they are set up by individuals looking to make a buck off of you. Many of these websites set you up with a so-called credit monitoring service, and then they charge you a monthly fee. It is my professional opinion that most of these are a big waste of money, so I would never endorse them. Do you really want to pay some guy working in his pajamas from his basement who set up a site that looks deceptively like the government or like a credit agency? I met a man in his twenties who set up a personal website that looked so official, his site was mentioned in a respected national newspaper. As a result, he was raking in the money. He had the biggest chuckle when he told me about it at a conference I attended in Arizona.

Be aware that the score available for purchase from the credit bureau website, annualcreditreport.com, is not the same score you get when you apply for a mortgage to buy a house. This is because they're using a more lenient mathematical algorithm. It is an equation used for credit card approval rather than for a mortgage approval. Naturally, there are stricter requirements to borrow $100,000 or more than for getting a little plastic card to shop with. Therefore, I do not recommend buying the consumer credit score.

How to Order Your Report Successfully the First Time

Following is a sample letter for ordering your credit report by mail. So that you don't have to type it out, you will find instructions on how to get all of the letter templates in a .doc file at the end of this book. That will save you time typing letters that I have already done for you.

Note: With your letter, please include a copy of photo ID (such as a driver's license) and a document that verifies your name and address (such as a utility bill or other bill). Even though it might seem like a hassle, ID is used to prevent fraud and identity theft. One of the excuses credit bureaus use to stall on fixing your credit is to say you did not provide proper identification, so don't let them use that on you.

HOW TO PROPERLY DISPUTE NEGATIVE ACCOUNTS

Another one of their excuses is, "We can't read the address on your driver's license." So get a large, clear copy of your ID.

You should not order your credit report by phone. It would be too easy for someone to impersonate you and then they would receive all your personal information. And remember, you must first order your current report (dated within the last 12 months) before you can dispute it.

On the following page is a letter you can download to request your report. Or if you prefer, you can print this form provided by the CPFB at http://1.usa.gov/1nAFeSy

Use a #10 business envelope only.

Your request will be processed within 15 days from the time they receive your letter.

You can request your report from all three credit bureaus at this one address:

Annual Credit Report Request Service

P.O. Box 105281

Atlanta, GA 30348-5281

Letter #1 To Request Your Credit Report By Mail

Please note: With this letter, include a copy of your photo ID (such as a driver's license) and one other document verifying your name and address, such as a utility or cable bill if you believe there might be an error address less than two years or if you believe there might be an error or confusion with your name, social security number, or address. By being proactive, you will prevent a delay in getting your report.

To receive this letter and all the other letters in this book as a .doc file so that you can fill in the appropriate spaces without having to retype the entire letters, see the quick and simple instructions in the Conclusion at the end of this book.

Your Name
Your Address
City, State Zip code
Date of Birth
Social Security #

Your previous address <if you have lived at your current address less than two years>
City, State Zip code

Annual Credit Report Request Service
P.O. Box 105281
Atlanta, GA 30348-5281

Date

Dear Credit Representative:
Please send me my free annual credit report.
Sincerely,
Your signature
<Type your name below your signature>

Step Two: Dispute the negative item with the credit bureau.

Be careful to dispute your negative item only with the credit bureaus that record it. For example, if your late payment with Visa shows up only on Equifax, then dispute it only with Equifax. You certainly don't want to stir up trouble with Experian and TransUnion where there is none! Remember, not all companies report to all three credit bureaus.

The easiest way to do this is to use the Credit Investigation Form. This form will come to you with the packet of letters in .doc form, so you don't have to re-create it. (It is not shown here, because it doesn't format well with the Kindle platform.)

By law, the credit bureaus must consider your request to investigate. If they cannot verify that the negative item is true, accurate, and complete, then they must delete it. The law is on your side. "Innocent unless proven guilty." The burden of proof is on them.

The credit bureau must respond to your request to investigate within 30 days (plus mail time). Either they will delete the negative entry from your credit report, or they will claim it has been verified as accurate. They delete it, you're happy! If they claim it has been verified, you go on to the next step. This is perfectly normal, so don't get bummed out and quit.

Use the address on the credit report you received by mail for sending in the Credit Investigation Request Form.

Many people have had great success with this form over the years. I've had loan officers ask me for this form to use for themselves. They have had old collections deleted, raised their scores, and the next thing I knew, they were calling me with the great news that they were buying a lovely home.

Step Three: Dispute the negative item with the company itself.

If the negative item you disputed came back "verified," it doesn't mean they really verified it. See Chapter 4, "What the Credit Bureaus Don't Want You to Know" for the inside scoop. For now, just know that your next step is to send a strong yet professional letter to the company (credit card provider, auto finance company, etc.). The burden of proof is on the company who is reporting the negative information, so they need to haul out their records from the archives and prove you were late or failed to make payment. If they don't do this, you are entitled to have the late payment deleted from your report.

Once they receive your letter, they must spring into action and respond within 30 to 45 days. It is illegal for them to ignore your letter, toss it aside, or forget about it. Accordingly, you should send the letter by Certified Mail. That way, they cannot claim it never arrived, because someone has to sign for it, and then the tag on the envelope comes back to you, so you have legal proof, just in case you need it. (More about that step later.)

I suggest using of one the letter templates I've prepared. This makes it super easy for you, because you fill in your personal information using the .doc template and print it out. You don't have to compose something out of thin air or type it all from scratch. There is no sense reinventing the wheel when these letters have already been proven to work. These letters are similar to the very same letters used by attorneys and credit restoration services. Everyone uses a variation of the same basic letter: it challenges the information, cites the law, and demands correction.

Warning: Don't make the fatal mistake of giving too much information. When a person calls the creditor or writes out the long story of what happened and why, they are sabotaging their success. Listen: no one at the creditor's office cares about you personally, so don't get into it. Don't write about your trials and tribulations. Don't tell about your doctor visits. Don't mention your children. And don't call the salespeople at the auto shop scumbags or other names. Just use the basic template, modifying it as needed.

"Can I personalize it?" you may ask. The answer is yes, as long as you do not admit fault or guilt. Do not say, "I made a mistake," "I didn't know better at the time," "my bookkeeper messed up," or "I was tricked and deceived." If you do, you are cementing the bad mark into your report and will not be able to get it deleted for a very, very long time. This is why a friend of mine, a top expert on credit restoration, refuses to take on a client who has been communicating in this way on his own first.

On the other hand, if you personalize the letter properly, you can help your cause. At the end of this chapter are some examples. However, if you are unsure, then simply use the template letter, filling in your own name, address, account number, etc.

After you complete this step, the creditor will either agree to delete the negative item or not. Either way, you will receive notice. At this point, many creditors will agree to deleting the negative item simply because they don't want to go through the hassle of digging up old records for proper verification. Time is money to them. Other times, they will agree to delete the negative item because they want to keep you as a customer, and they figure they will come out ahead financially by making you happy so that you keep spending money at their store. This is good business sense, and it is within their legal right.

Unfortunately, some stubborn company employees will come back saying the negative item was true, correct, and it remains on your report. Don't despair if this happens. It happens every day in the attorney and credit repair company offices, and they don't despair or give up. They simply move on to step four, and that is what you're going to do also.

Step Four: Demand written proof, called Debt Validation.

If they don't want to extend courteous customer service and agree to delete a past mistake so that you can get on with your life, then you have the legal right to demand a Debt Validation.

This step is going to be inconvenient for them, which is good for you! The Fair Debt Collection Protection Act is a law that gives you the right to receive the following five documents:

1) An explanation of what the alleged debt is for. This is so you receive assurance that the so-called debt really does belong to you.

2) A complete payment history of the account that includes the calculations showing how they arrived at the balance. This is so you have proof that the amount they claim is owed is the correct amount.

3) A copy of the agreement or signed credit application that shows you agreed to pay this debt. This is so you have proof it belongs to you, as opposed to someone else with the same name or perhaps someone who forged your signature.

4) A copy of the agreement that grants the collection agency authority to collect on the aged debt. This applies if the debt has been sold to a third party agency, which they do have the right to do.

5) A copy of the creditor's state license, including their license number. This is so you know they are a valid company and not some scammer overseas who is trying to get your money illegally.

Following is a sample letter you can use for requesting a Debt Validation. (It is included in the letter packet in .doc form for your easy use.)

You will see that this letter also says, "Stop contacting me about this or any other matter you have, except to provide me with accurate verification of this debt by U.S. mail only." When you say this, they

HOW TO PROPERLY DISPUTE NEGATIVE ACCOUNTS

must stop calling you on the phone and communicate only via mail. This will cut down on the harassment and stress you have to endure.

Be sure to open all your mail and pay attention to it. Letting letters pile up, unopened, could end up putting you in serious legal trouble and cost you even more money in the end.

Sample Letter Requesting Debt Validation

Your Name
Your Address
City, State Zip code

Collection Company
Address
City, State Zip code

Date

Re: Account # <fill in>

Dear Collector:

My credit report shows a collection from your agency. I was never notified of this collection. What's more, I do not believe this debt is accurate. Under the FAIR DEBT COLLECTION PROTECTION ACT, I have the right to request and receive validation of the debt. Therefore, please provide me with a copy of the following:

- An explanation of what this alleged account balance is for.
- A calculation of this balance, including the complete payment history on this account, so I have proof that the amount is correct.
- Documentation that shows I agreed to pay this debt.
- The Agreement that grants you authority to collect on this alleged debt.
- A copy of your state license, including license number.

Stop contacting me about his or any other matter you have, except to provide me with accurate verification of this debt by U.S. mail only.

Sincerely,
<Sign the letter>
Your name typed

IMPORTANT POINT If a creditor fails to provide you with proper debt validation, they cannot report it (or continue to report it) to the credit bureaus, they are not allowed to collect money from you, they are not allowed to call or contact you about the debt. If they report a false, unverifiable debt to the credit bureaus, it is a violation of FACTA. This law states you can then sue for $1,000 in damages for each violation.

You may sue in small claims court without the expense of an attorney, or you may sue in a state or federal court if the amount is too large for small claims.

Collection Company Gets Sued and Agrees to Settle for $240,000

In Houston, Texas, a collection company by the name of United Recovery Systems, Inc. rushed to settle a lawsuit before it had a chance to go to court. Naturally, they didn't admit guilt, but they agreed to pay $240,000, which I think says a lot in itself. Not only was United Recovery Systems, Inc. sued for failing to provide Debt Validation, but they were also sued for the unkind and threatening things said to people when they called them. So, their nastiness caught up with them. (You can locate the article on the FTC.gov website by doing a Google search of "United Recovery Systems" + $240,000)

By the way, do not let a collector verbally abuse or harass you. Doing so is illegal, and you have the law on your side. On the flip side, don't you yell or cuss at them, either. Keep your communication businesslike and don't get personal. Remember, you are going to handle your credit repair like a pro, not an amateur.

Step Five: Follow Up with the Credit Bureaus

If the creditor fails to properly validate your debt, use the letter on the following page to send to the credit bureaus, taking care to send only to the bureaus that report this specific debt. According to law, the bureau must delete the debt that has not been validated.

When this happens, your credit score will immediately go up. Depending on what the rest of your credit report looks like, your score might increase by 40, 60, or even more points.

Sample Letter Following Up with a Credit Bureau After the Creditor Failed to Provide You with a Proper Debt Validation

Credit Bureau
PO Box
City, State, Zip code
Date

Re: Account # <fill in number>

Dear Credit Representative:

I am disputing the account stated above. Previously, I disputed this account information as being inaccurate, and you responded by stating you were able to verify this debt. But how is that possible? Under the laws of the FDCPA, I have contacted the collection agency <name the company> myself, and they have failed to verify that this is indeed my debt.

I enclose copies of my requests to the collection agency, asking them to validate the debt, as well as the receipts showing I sent this letter by certifed signature request. I was given no evidence of my obligation to pay this debt to this collection agency. This debt is not mine.

The Fair Credit Reporting act requires you to verify the validity of this within 30 days. If the validity cannot be verified, you are obligated by law to remove it from my credit file. I urge you to remove this account before I am forced to take legal action.

In the event that you cannot verify the item pursuant to FCRA, and you continue to report it on my credit, I will find it necessary to sue you for actual damages and declaratory relief. According to FCRA regulations, I may sue you in any qualified state or federal court, including small claims court in my area.

I look forward to a swift and amicable resolution to this matter.

Sincerely,
<sign the letter>
Your name typed

CHAPTER 3

How Fast (and How Much) Will Your Credit Score Improve?

I had a client, Bruce, a professional with a high income who wanted to buy a house near his place of work in Seattle. When I pulled his credit, I saw that all his credit cards and auto loan were paid on time, but he had a shockingly low score. The reason is that he had a page filled with petty collections. The amounts were $16, $25, $47, $30, and so on. All were under a hundred dollars. It was crazy, because he had an excellent income. When I asked him what was going on, he said they were parking tickets for downtown Seattle. I instructed him to use the method in this book to get rid of those mistakes. (And not to accrue anymore!) Bruce got to work, and in less than 90 days, the annoying collections were "washed away," his score shot up by 112 points, and he was easily approved to buy a pretty cool house that his Realtor found.

The good news for you is that the moment a late payment, collection, or other negative item is deleted from your credit, your score instantly goes up. Also, the moment the credit bureaus record a lower balance on a high balance credit card, your score goes up.

If you have a late payment from five years ago deleted, you can expect your score to go up by 10 points. If you have a recent late payment deleted, your score may go up by 100 points. Thus, we see the age of the late payment is significant.

Here is more about how it works.

No one is watching your credit or calculating your score day by day. There are approximately 52 million Americans with credit records, so that would be impossible to do.

When a bank or other creditor pulls your credit report, that is when your score is automatically calculated by the computerized mathematical system, at that very moment. So if your report showed a collection yesterday and now it has been deleted, your score will be higher today than it would have been yesterday. In that regard, you could say that the results are instantaneous.

However, you must allow time for the process. When you send a letter of dispute, the Fair Credit Reporting Act gives the creditor 30 days to respond. To this, add days for the mail to go back and forth. If they cooperate with your request, you will receive a letter stating the item has been deleted. At this point, you make copies of the letter to send to the bureaus. (Always keep your original letters. These are like gold to you!) Even though the creditor is supposed to update the bureaus, I suggest that you do what the pros do: send the update yourself, because you can't always trust the creditor to work on your behalf in a timely manner.

The credit bureaus update your electronic file once a month. If you send in your request two days before their update schedule, you'll see fast results; but if your request was sent in 29 days before their update schedule, you'll have to wait almost a month. Because we don't know which day of the month they are scheduled to update the information on your file, we have to assume 30 days for the update to take place.

Credit repair specialists say that six to eight months is a fair window to allow for credit restoration, for most of their clients. If you have only one or two accounts to dispute, then you might see results in as little as two months. For more difficult situations that involve a bankruptcy or foreclosure, it can take more than a year.

We all want to know *exactly* how the numbers work for that complex 40-component algorithm. I have included a partial scorecard for you to see—something you cannot find on the Internet. This has never been offered to the public. It's a secret guarded like national security.

How many points will your score increase by having collections deleted?

The answer depends on what the rest of your credit report looks like. Let's look at three scenarios.

1. If your report is good and you have a score of 620, and if you have two collections deleted, your score could go up to 680 or even 700.

2. If your report has other negative elements, such as a lot of high credit card balances, and your score is 580, then your score might up to 620 or 640. But when you pay down your balances to lower your balance-to-limit ratio, you score might increase by 40 or 50 points.

3. If you have a page of collections deleted, your score might have an increase of 100 to 120 pints.

So you can see that there is not a set number of points assigned to a collection so that everyone's score increases by that exact amount when the collection is deleted. The system is much more complex than that.

Furthermore, which month or which week or even which day your credit is pulled can make a difference. Part of the credit scoring method is based on a grading curve, so it depends what is happening with the rest of the population and how you compare with them *at the moment* your credit is pulled and scored.

Then to make it even more complicated and unpredictable, there are "slots" for processing your credit score. On one day, your file might fall into "slot one," and on another day, it might randomly fall into "slot nine," creating more variation.

What this means is that no one can tell you exactly how many points your credit score is going to change. So beware of advertisers or salespeople who make exact claims. Getting rid of a collection account will not result in the same number of points for everyone. The scoring system looks at your whole picture and at the whole picture of society, and then it has additional variables as well. The important thing is that we do know enough so that we can *take control* of our own credit and earn ourselves a respectable score.

IMPORTANT POINT Bad credit is only a temporary situation when you take control of your credit rating. You *can* fix the mistakes of the past and make a better future for yourself.

Coming Up Next

Information that the credit bureaus would like to sweep under the rug and hide from the public. This is the stuff they'd really prefer you not to know.

CHAPTER 4

What the Credit Bureaus Don't Want You to Know

If the credit bureaus had their way, you would believe exactly what they tell you, no questions asked. But please, don't fall into their trap.

Chances are, your credit report contains one or more errors, and those errors are negatively impacting your life. Check out these statistics revealed by a study conducted by the national Association of State Public Interest Research Groups:

- 79% of all credit reports contain some type of error.

- 54% contain inaccurate personal information, such as a misspelled name, incorrect birth date, wrong social security number, or out-of-date address. For example, one man's business partner was listed on his report as his spouse.

- 30% listed paid off and closed accounts as being open. (This can either hurt or help your score, depending.)

- 22% had the same loan listed twice. (This skews the debt-to-income ratio against you. Even worse, if there are duplicate late payments, your score is penalized twice. Included in the packet of letters is one you can use to have a duplicate account removed.)

- 8% omitted a major credit card, loan, or a mortgage that would have provided positive credit and boosted the person's score, if it had been included.

This is an outrage! Can you imagine if the work you did contained errors 79% of the time? How fast would you be put on step one, step two, and then booted out the door? So why are the credit bureaus making so many errors on our credit files?

It is because about 30,000 data entry clerks process 4.5 billion pieces of credit information each and every month. If there is a 1% error factor, that would result in 45 million errors, per month. Wow.

The reason it is important for you to know this information is so that you have the confidence to challenge the accuracy of your own credit report. You need to understand that you are not doing anything weird or uncalled for when you challenge their accuracy.

The Law Steps In

With so many errors penalizing innocent people, the U.S. government was forced to step in and enact laws to protect its citizens. So you see, the intent of the law is to protect you, not to force you into keeping the negative information set in stone "from now till kingdom come." Here are some highlights that you should know:

- If there is an error, the negative information **must be deleted.**

- If it cannot be proven or verified, the negative information **must be deleted.**

- If grace or pardon is extended by the creditor, the negative information **must be deleted.**

- If a creditor wants to keep you as a customer and they think it will make you happy and encourage you to continue to do business with their company, the negative information **may be deleted.** So yes, it is legal.

Understandably, the credit bureaus don't like people disputing their records. It costs them money to hire employees to handle all these disputes. According to their own published information, they seem to want you to believe all negative accounts must be reported on your credit report for seven years. But this is not true! The truth is that late payments "can" or "may" be reported for seven years, not "must" be reported. The truth is that accounts don't have to be reported at all!

Some companies choose not to report to the credit bureaus, because it is voluntary, not mandatory. Funny how some people try to say "it's the law" that your late payment had to be reported, isn't it?

Dirty Little Secret

People with low credit scores have their credit pulled on average 17 times, compared with just one time for the people with good credit. For every credit pull, the bureaus make money. Is it any wonder they're happy to keep your scores low?

Little Known Fact

Another exasperating fact is that some of the credit disputes are outsourced to third world countries where labor is cheaper. So here's the scene: a young person in India who has never been to the U.S. or had an account in the U.S. is reading your dispute and deciding your fate. She or he makes a judgment call, and who's to know if it is correct? I mean, how much could they possibly know about the American credit system or about your personal situation?

It Gets Worse

Another outrage is that in the United States, the bureaus hire inexperienced employees at minimum wage to handle disputes—and then they put the employees under tremendous pressure to process a certain number of dispute letters per hour and per day. This means they are forced to make a quick decision if they want to keep their jobs. These people don't have the experience, critical acumen, mature judgment, *or the time* to properly research your account. They whip through your request as fast as they can, and then it's like, "Next!"

If you'd like to read more about this, Bob Sullivan has thoroughly documented these practices in his excellent book titled, *Your Evil Twin: Behind the Identity Theft Epidemic* (Wiley & Sons Pub.)

For example, on page 98 he writes: "One representative at Experian explains in a deposition that when she began working at the firm, agents were required to handle 62 calls per day, but within a couple of years, the quotas had increased to 100 complaint calls per day, leaving them only an average of 3 to 4 minutes per call. The quotas were strictly enforced, and representatives were told they could lose their jobs for failing to handle an adequate number of calls. During training, customer service representatives were specifically taught to mistrust consumers. Moreover, one customer service representative explained that Experian's call center would block an individual's number who called too many times."

IMPORTANT POINT Keep a copy of the letters you send, just in case you need them in a court of law or to refer to later. Avoid using the telephone for disputes, except in super-simple, one-item cases.

Why Do They Keep Their Address Hidden?

If you've ever tried finding a mailing address on the official website owned by the credit bureaus (annualcreditreport.com), you've discovered that there is no address posted. They are pushing everyone to order online—and the reason is *not for your convenience!* The three bureaus have three different post office box numbers—and they change their P.O. box numbers from time to time. This delays people's attempts at disputing, because a good number of letters get sent back to the senders.

To order your reports, use the address in Chapter 2. To dispute an item, use the address of the credit bureau on your credit report.

Coming Up Next

The ads by the nonprofit credit counseling groups who pretend to be on your side are deceiving. This is information you'll want to pass on to your friends and family so they don't get tricked.

CHAPTER 5

What Credit Counseling Groups Don't Want

You to Know

When I was new in the mortgage business, I got in a bit of trouble with my boss, all because I didn't know any better than to believe an advertisement I heard on the radio.

A lady had called in to apply for a home loan. When I saw that she had many large balance collection accounts and a very low score, I could not get her approved even back in the lenient subprime lending days. The sum of her collection accounts was far more than she and her husband could afford to pay off. It looked like it would take half a lifetime for them to dig out of their financial hole. So remembering the radio ad and mistakenly thinking that *nonprofit* automatically meant *good guys on your side*, I suggested they call Consumer Credit Counseling Service to negotiate their debt. A few short days later, my manager called me into her office.

"Did you refer the X family to CCCS?" she asked in an angry voice.

"Yes," I said and explained why.

"Don't you ever do that again! I got a call from Bob today. (The manager of a collection company a few miles away. Turns out Bob and my manager are business colleagues.) He is livid that Mrs. X said she's not going to pay the account, because CCC is taking care of it. His collection company DOES NOT WORK WITH CCCS!" Now her face was even redder than before.

37

"I'm sorry, I didn't know," I said, taken aback and still befuddled.

"Consumer Credit Counseling and other debt management companies like them make matters worse than they already are. The creditors report to the bureaus that the account is being handled by a debt management company. We, and all lenders, regard this the same as being in a Chapter 13 bankruptcy."

"Really? Why is that?"

"Because it is a big statement that says they could not manage their own money. They cannot get a mortgage until they complete the program and are out of it. Furthermore, it lowers their credit score."

I was horrified. And embarrassed. I promised never to do it again. She made me go apologize to Bob in person. It was awful.

Later, I saw credit reports that belonged to people who had been in debt management programs. The entire time they were in the program, the credit card companies reported them as **not** "paid as agreed," because the program negotiates lower payments. This shows up on their reports as **late** month after month after month.

It absolutely trashed their credit scores.

The people said, "But we paid on time every month. The debt counselor never told us this would happen. We thought working with their service was helping us."

Three things mortgage lenders don't like to see on a credit report: A bankruptcy, a debt management service, and a foreclosure. They are all poison.

I took an informal poll among mortgage lenders. "Which is better and less harmful: filing bankruptcy or going to Consumer Credit Counseling?" I asked.

All but one said it was better and less harmful to file a Chapter 7 bankruptcy.

One mortgage account executive put it succinctly, "Better to file Chapter 7 and get it over with in 90 days than to drag in on and on with Consumer Credit Counseling, which looks just as bad."

Some lenders will not approve a loan application while you are in a debt consolidation program, for the same reason they won't approve a loan while you're in the middle of a bankruptcy.

Consumer Credit Counseling companies act like a middleman. Many of them make 15% profit from your creditors, even though they have a nonprofit status. I call them wolves in sheep's clothing.

It is my opinion that 98 percent of the people are better off negotiating their own payment modification. That way, they can get the agreement in writing that says the new, lower payment will be considered "paid as agreed." Moreover, they will not have the words "account in consumer debt program" damaging their reputations for the whole world to see.

Coming Up Next

It might seem like a good idea to use a lawyer to work on your credit report; however, I never recommend a law firm for this type of work. I explain why next.

CHAPTER 6

What the Lawyers Don't Want You to Know

I like attorneys for times when you really need an attorney. They're expensive, but they are worth the cost for those times, such as when you've been accused of committing a murder when you're completely innocent. If that happened, most of us would pay a lot of money to hire an expert lawyer to prove our innocence and keep us out of prison.

But you don't need an attorney to fix your credit. It is my personal opinion that the vast majority of law firms are not the best option for this job. My viewpoint comes from working as an agent for a private credit restoration service that has a higher success rate than any attorney I've ever seen. And in my work as a mortgage account executive and as a loan officer, I've seen hundreds of credit reports.

One thing lawyers don't want you to know is that they stand to make $500/hour on you as a client. Sure, they might advertise "$49/month," but come on, have you ever seen an attorney who works for $49 an hour? Or even $49 for half-an-hour? *Never!*

So exactly how much personal attorney attention do you think you're going to get per month for that fee? One attorney said he takes "mere minutes per month," because he uses his computer software program. This is the same attorney that says right on his website that it is "easy to make $500 an hour doing credit repair."

So what happens is that the computer spits out form letters that are successful in getting the super easy bad credit off your report—the stuff that you could hire a high school kid to do. He takes his sweet time about sending off all the letters, too. That way, the months roll by and he collects more monthly fees.

41

How long is it going to take to get through your entire credit report? Two years? Ten? A lifetime? This is why I don't suggest taking a monthly plan. One flat fee gives the attorney incentive to get the job done faster so you can get on with your life.

Another Inside Secret

Attorneys who do credit work like to set up people on auto-pay. This is not for your convenience. It is because a lot of people with bad credit are chronic late payers. But there's more to it. These people who let bills slide also won't get around to canceling the auto-pay. They are chronic procrastinators. This works to the attorney's advantage.

One young gentleman came to me for a home loan when I worked for a mortgage broker in Seattle. He'd been set up on auto-pay with Lexington Law for years. Yes, years! He still had a couple collections on his report that they couldn't get rid of (although they did improve his credit). He said, "I just never got around to canceling the auto-pay."

For the past year, not one iota of progress had been made on his credit. "I guess I should get around to canceling," he said.

Well yes. That would save him hundreds of dollars per year.

The reality is that an ultra-cheap attorney fee is not a bargain. It is not going to buy you any significant quality time with the lawyer. Personally, I know two certified credit repair specialists—one on the East Coast and one on the West Coast—who do better, more thorough, faster work than any credit lawyer I've ever seen. (To receive their names and contact information, send me a message through my website, www.askcarolynwarren.com.)

Coming Up Next

Credit repair specialists have their secrets too. In the next chapter, I tell you what questions you should ask and how to search out the good guys from the bad.

CHAPTER 7

What Credit Repair Companies Don't Want You to Know

How would you feel about having an inexperienced person handle your credit repair—for a high fee? Well guess what? That is exactly what has happened to a lot of trusting people. Here's the how and why.

You see a great-looking website about credit repair. You call and ask how many years' experience the so-called expert has. He or she says, "Fifteen years." That sounds good to you. But what you don't know is that this person actually has only one or two years' experience doing actual credit repair work. The other 14 years' experience were working as a loan officer. Because mortgage and credit go hand-in-hand, and because he or she has been reading credit reports for that long, he or she feels justified in telling you this lie.

Since 2007, many loan officers have lost their jobs. Doing credit repair is one of the industries some have chosen to go into. Even worse, other entrepreneurs, former sales people in other industries, have also decided to take up credit repair. As a result, brand new companies have sprung up as fast as they can put up a website. Some people purchased credit repair franchises, so they claim to be "ten years in the business," because the company itself is that old, not that they have that experience themselves.

An attorney who specializes in credit repair is now selling his credit repair software to loan officers and other entrepreneurs who want to get into the business. And think about this: If it's such a great business, why is the attorney selling his program, creating more competition for himself? Wouldn't he want to keep all the clients he could? Especially since he advertises that he spends "mere minutes a month" on each credit client?

I am not against hiring a good, reputable company that has at least five years' *real, hands-on* experience. Some people don't have the time to devote to fixing their credit, and they do have the funds to hire a professional. I'm just saying to exercise caution by doing your research first so you don't find out a year later that you've shelled out cash only to receive very little results.

How to Check Out a Potential Credit Repair Company

- Check out their Better Business Bureau membership at www.bbb.org. However, I don't give a lot of weight on this. The BBB is more than happy to remove bad marks for the companies that pay their ridiculously expensive membership fee, so they are not a truly unbiased source.

- See if there are complaints posted about the company at www.RipOffReport.com.

- Do a Google search to see if complaints show up on forums and check Yelp.com.

There is no substitute for experience, especially in the area of credit. Never sign up with a company over the Internet without first speaking with the credit repair specialist on the phone.

Do you want to be smooth-talked into a commitment by a slick salesperson and then find out later that the attorney is spending "mere minutes per month" on your credit file?

In addition, take a close look at their website. Take the time to actually read through the verbiage, not just glance at the overall photos and lay-out. You might find a website, as I did, that claims the credit expert has a college degree in finance—and yet his website is full of

English errors. He uses bad grammar, such as "me and Tom." He spells "gets" as "get's" to name just a couple blatant errors that anyone who actually earned a college degree should not be committing. Personally, I don't trust websites with spelling and English errors. Is that the kind of person you want writing your letters to the creditors? And who are these people *really*? Are they even in the United States of America, or are they operating out of an Internet café in a third world country?

Beware of False Guarantees

If a credit repair company guarantees you certain results, that is a giant red flag that says something is amiss. No one can guarantee what the credit bureaus will do, so such guarantees are deceptive. On the other hand, if they guarantee to put forth their best effort, that is fine. However, I would expect any true professional to put forth their best effort without "guaranteeing" it.

Coming Up Next

The Federal Trade Commission is supposed to look out for the best interests of the citizens of the U.S. So why are they posting information that is untrue?

CHAPTER 8

What the Federal Trade Commission Doesn't Want You to Know

I applaud the Federal Trade Commission (FTC) for the good work they do in protecting Americans from fraud. I am happy that they expose common credit repair scams. But I am not happy about the blatant falsehoods they try to foist on the public. I'll explain.

Two Scams Exposed

Here are two common scams the FTC wants you to avoid (as do I). But there's a twist that the FTC is not telling you.

1) Temporary credit repair.

Shoddy credit repair companies send in a letter to dispute your bad credit, which is the first step after receiving and analyzing the credit report. U.S. law allows for a 30-day investigation period and requires that a negative item cannot be included in calculating your credit score during the investigation period, because if it is false, that would unfairly penalize you. As I explained earlier, some disputed items come off at first request, but others stay on so that you must proceed with step 2, step 3, and step 4. But these shoddy companies quit after step one.

So what happens is that you pay them their $500 or $1,000 fee, they send off one letter to the bureaus, a couple negative items are deleted, and the rest of the negative items pop back onto your report after the 30-day investigation period. The shoddy credit repair company doesn't do any more work for you, so you have basically wasted your money. It's a rip-off, and I'm glad the FTC exposes it by educating people about temporary credit repair.

But here's the twist: A competent credit repair company does not accept temporary credit repair. They keep a record of each negative item that was deleted, then if the credit bureau tries to re-post it, they send a letter of complaint that states the date the item was deleted (which shows it was deemed inappropriate to be posted), and they demand that it be removed again, this time *permanently*. After all, this is the law, and the bureaus must be held to the law! If the bureau removes an account that they deemed to be false previously, and then they re-post it later, it is like they are convicting you twice. They can't do that. Once a person has been pronounced innocent, they cannot be tried again for the same crime. The best professionals use this law to make sure your credit repair is permanent, not temporary. They follow-up as needed and don't let the bureaus get away with re-posting a negative item they once took off. If you are doing your own credit repair, you will need to take this step as well, just as the pros do.

So when the FTC says, "Credit repair is temporary," they are not telling you the whole story. A half-truth is not the truth.

2) Creating a new identity.

This scam is even worse that the first. It's not just a rip-off, it is also illegal and can land you in trouble with the law, being prosecuted for fraud, which is a serious crime. How it works is that the so-called "credit doctor" offers to create a new social security number so that you can get a "fresh start." There are also books that instruct you to create a new social security number for yourself, that way, your bad credit is no longer attached to your name. It follows your old (real) social security number and you skate off with a new slate. Doing this could add prison time to your troubles, so don't be tempted. I am glad the FTC exposes this fraud as well.

Refuse to Believe the Lie!

After doing their good work of exposing scams, why does the FTC have to go on and publish a lie? Just when they get you to thinking

48

they're the Good Guys looking out for your protection, they slip in some false information. And I'm sorry, but I have a hard time believing that they don't know any better.

Here is a quote from the FTC that includes a false statement in the last two lines:

"Credit-repair schemes are a big problem for consumers," says Eileen Harrington, deputy director of the Federal Trade Commission's Bureau of Consumer Protection, which is leading a federal crackdown on these crooks. 'Credit-repair promoters generally charge hundreds of dollars, but don't deliver on their claims. The fact is, they can't. No one can legally remove accurate and timely information from your credit report."

Her "fact" is no fact at all! The real truth is that credit repair services, attorneys, creditors themselves, and private citizens can and do legally remove accurate and timely negative information from credit reports. It is happening every business day of the week. I've done it, I've seen other loan officers do it, I've seen good credit repair and credit restoration services do it, and I've seen proof that attorneys do it. I have also seen private citizens do it themselves as well. For example, a woman from Norway who had immigrated to the U.S. discovered she had a collection on her credit report when she went to refinance. She had no idea she had this one overdue account as the creditor had not been contacting her. She came to me for advice, and I told her the same method I am sharing with you in this book. Not long after, she came back to me with the good news that the collection had disappeared, her score rose, and she completed her refinance.

Be assured: people (like you) *do* get bad credit removed.

So why is the FTC trying to make you believe it can't be done? Why is their spokeswoman saying, "The fact is they can't (remove bad credit)?" Why is she lying to the public?

49

Then to add to the annoyance, reporters and journalists and websites quote and repeat this big lie that says bad credit can't be removed. When the public reads it over and over again and see that the statement is from the FTC, they believe it—and who can blame them?

Make no mistake: the statement by the FTC is not true. And for the record, I will accept an interview with every journalist who contacts me. I love to speak with the media to help them get the truth out.

As if that's not enough, here is another quote from the FTC that is based on the big lie quoted above: "Only time, a conscious effort and a personal debt-repayment plan can improve your credit report."

That is exactly what the credit bureaus want you to believe: that you're stuck until time drags by, taking your last breath of hope with it. But hold on! There is no law that says a business cannot delete your late payment early if they choose to do so. And they do! Why? Because it makes good business sense. When they give you what's called a "good faith adjustment" and forgive your late payment, it makes you love them and continue to spend money with them. They come out ahead by spreading goodwill. Since they own your account information, they can do this. And plenty of them do, every day. It is 100 percent legal. Remember, the law did not require them to report the late payment in the first place. So they can instruct the bureaus to take it off if they so choose.

Now here's some more BAD advice based on a half-truth/half-lie from the FTC: "There isn't anything a credit-repair firm can do for you for a fee that you can't do for yourself for free. So avoid any company that wants you to pay for such services, especially before they provide them. That too is against the law."

Yes, it's true that you can do the work for yourself that a credit repair firm would do for you. You can follow the steps outlined in Chapter 2 and the rest of the book. But some people are super busy and have the finances to hire a professional. Some people are working 60 hours a week, so they'd much prefer to hire a certified credit specialist than to do the work themselves.

Likewise, some people prefer to hire a landscaping company rather than dig, plant, fertilize, water, and weed themselves. Just because you *could* landscape your own yard for free, does it mean that all landscape services are scammers? Of course not. They are providing a valuable service for busy people and for people who don't have a penchant for working outdoors with plants. Why doesn't the FTC say, "There isn't anything a lawn mower can do for you for a fee that you can't do for yourself for free. So avoid any lawn mower that wants you to pay for such services"?

Similarly, there is nothing against the law about hiring a service to write your letters and do the negotiations for you. It is NOT against the law to hire a professional service. Look at all the services people hire that they could do themselves: automobile oil change, child care, manicure and pedicure services, income tax services, and on and on. You can see why I get really steamed up by these falsehoods!

Again, good on the FTC for exposing fraud, but please stop already with your so-called warnings about the legal credit repair. Stop purporting that it can't be done, when it is being done—and you know it.

Fact: credit repair is legal in all 50 states. This is confirmed by state law and by licensed attorneys and certified credit specialists who perform this type of service.

Coming Up Next

What the pros know about credit scoring that you should know, too.

CHAPTER 9

The Inside Scoop on Credit Scoring

Imagine you're a contestant on *The Price is Right* with the giant wheel and host Drew Carey. Drew says, "Spin the wheel! The number that comes up is your credit score!"

While you're reeling from shock, he goes on to say, "If you spin a 740, you can buy a luxury home and get the cheapest financing. But if your marker lands on 610, watch out, because greedy sharks will come at you with hungry appetites to gobble up as much of your money as they can. And if you're really unlucky and spin a 480, then you can forget about having any kind of financial success at all."

That would be a really rotten game show. And yet, that's what it feels like when you don't understand how the credit scoring system works. You've been told that the almighty credit score dictates whether or not you can buy a car or home of your own and what your interest rate will be. John R. Ulzheimer, who spent 16 years working as a credit industry insider for Equifax and FICO, wrote this in his excellent book, *You're Nothing but a Number:*

"The credit reporting agencies have more influence over your life than any other company. They are simply the most powerful companies in the United States."

This is true, because most financial dealings depend on the credit score system. Understanding how credit scoring works is no longer optional—it is mandatory for financial success. You must control your score. No more gambling on the big wheel of luck!

Now is the time to take back some of the power from the uber-rich credit bureaus. When you understand the credit scoring system, you can literally control your own credit rating. You don't depend on banks, credit card providers, or anyone else, and you certainly don't depend on the spin of a wheel.

Using your new knowledge, you can make the right moves to gain credit points and stop doing those things that penalize points. You can also take the initiative to fix mistakes of the past.

Owning a high credit scores saves you many thousands of dollars in interest charges, loan fees, and insurance premiums. What's more, you gain confidence for making financial negotiations, because all business want to make transactions with people who have excellent credit. You receive approvals faster and easier than ever before. You gain respect from everyone you do business with. You are a good testimony to your family name and even to your faith.

As an encouragement, I'll share another success story with you.

Another Success Story

Henry, a personal friend of mine, wanted to improve his credit score. Due to some investments that went bad, Henry had acquired late payments and collection accounts. Although he had paid off his collections, he still had a low credit score, in the mid-500s. Consequently, the mortgage on his home was at 9.25%. Then he took control. With my counseling, he was able to send letters that got the late payments and collections removed from his credit reports. His score rose to top tier (over 740). He then refinanced into a 4.25% mortgage, lowering the rate he was paying to the lender by 5 percent. What a difference!

On a $200,000 mortgage, that savings calculates to be $661 per month. It saves $7,932 in the first year alone. After a couple years,

Henry sold that home and purchased a newer, larger home in a better neighborhood that suited his growing family.

What Exactly is a Credit Score?

Everyone talks about the credit score, so now is the time to understand exactly what it is.

Your credit score is a number between about 400 and 850 that grades you on your credit worthiness *The credit score is an index of risk*. It is an unbiased indicator of whether or not a consumer will repay a loan on time.

The score changes as new information is added to or deleted from the credit file. On the day your credit report is pulled, the scorecard instantly tabulates your score by the information available *at that moment*.

The score is based on all the credit-related data, not only on the negative data. Your established patterns of credit and payment correspond to the likelihood that you will make your payments on time or "as agreed" (to use their verbiage) in the future.

The following is a quotation from ""Explaining Experian," a document produced by Experian itself:

"Statistical analysis of data is used to define the characteristics (variables) that are most predictive of a consumer's future behavior. A scorecard typically contains a list of 15 to 20 characteristics each of which is assigned points that reflect whether it is a positive or negative indicator of future behavior. Usually, the characteristics that are associated with high risk result in an applicant losing points, while those linked to likely good performance (number of accounts paid on time, for example) will gain points. When the points for all the characteristics are added together, the result is the final score for each individual."

How Do the Bureaus Acquire Information About You?

Credit card companies, mortgage and finance companies, banks, collection agencies, catalog companies, magazine publishers, telephone companies, rental agencies, and more, report payment data to credit repositories. Not all creditors report to all three bureaus; thus, your score varies from Equifax to Experian to TransUnion.

You might be shocked when you read this quotation, also from "Explaining Experian," produced by Experian:

"Experian has a collection of databases that provide geographic, demographic, financial and lifestyle information on millions of consumers around the world... This information allows Experian to offer highly targeted lists of potential customers to our clients and to enhance the information held by them about their existing customers. Clients (companies) seeking consumer information can make selections based on the profiles of their most profitable customers or select from special lists, such as new parents, new homeowners or investors."

Wow, did you know they have a list of new parents and new homeowners? And that they sell your name and private information to companies so they can solicit you for sales? As an example of this, Experian said Crate and Barrel, a retailer of household goods and furniture, used Experian to obtain a list of avid catalog shoppers. They then sent catalogs to those people. Crate and Barrel also got email addresses from Experian. It seems the credit bureaus are making money every which way by collecting and selling our private information.

Back When Credit Scoring was Simpler

Originally, credit scoring was called "bankruptcy scoring." Lenders wanted to evaluate their risk of loaning money to you. The loan officer had a paper scorecard with which to evaluate your chances of going bankrupt. He or she asked you questions, checked the boxes with a ballpoint pen, and then added up your score at the bottom of the page. How quaint, right?

Then in 1996, computerized credit scoring became the standard for loan approval. The California-based Fair Isaac Company created a complex mathematical algorithm by analyzing millions of credit histories and using up to 40 variables. His numeric scoring system enabled consistent, impartial evaluation of loan requests. It showed itself to be astonishingly accurate in predicting the risk of granting credit—most of the time. Of course, if you happened to be one of the exceptions to that, then the scoring system became maddeningly unfair.

You Don't Get the Same Report the Mortgage Lenders Get

Traditionally, when you request a credit report from Experian, Equifax, or TransUnion, a special consumer format is given, without scores. By contrast, lenders and banks receive a report in a more complete format with a score page that assigns you a numeric score and four reasons why the score is not higher than it is.

December 4, 2003, President Bush signed into law the right of every citizen to receive one free credit report per year. The intent was to protect people from identity theft and from having inaccurate information posted about them.

Don't waste your time ordering a credit report from some random website that offers "free" reports. They are often incomplete and/or inaccurate. The score you receive might be artificially high, sometimes by 50 to 80 points. Instead, order from www.myannualcreditreport. com or get a copy of your report from your loan officer.

Coming Up Next

Why is the automobile industry using your credit score to set your auto insurance premiums? Shouldn't your safe driving status determine how much you pay for auto insurance rather than how you pay your credit cards? Is this a rip-off? These questions are answered next.

CHAPTER 10

Credit Scoring and the Automobile Industry

Tracy was angry when she learned that her insurance company was charging her more for auto insurance, not because she'd been in an accident, but because her credit score was not top tier.

"My bankruptcy has nothing to do with my driving. It's not fair!" she exclaimed. She is not alone in her protest. Many drivers wonder why insurance companies are offering discounts based on credit scores. They ask if it's some kind of scam.

The surprising fact is that studies have proven that credit scores are an accurate indicator of a person's likelihood of getting a traffic violation. As it turns out, people who have a lifestyle of paying creditors recklessly also drive recklessly.

Statistics also show that people who pay creditors meticulously (on time) also drive meticulously (obeying speed and other road rules); therefore, they have a lower incidence of citations and accidents. It's quite interesting how a person's attitude toward managing money has been found to mirror their attitude on the road.

A company called Choice Point collects, records, and sells information about people's insurance claim histories. The information is put into a report called the CLUE Report. (CLUE is an acronym for Comprehensive Loss Underwriting Exchange.)

An insurance agent for PEMCO Auto Insurance revealed the following score-based discounts:

Credit Score	Discount on Auto Insurance
725 – over	25% discount
625 – 724	17%
525 – 624	10%
524 – below	No discount

Knowing how credit scores are tied to auto insurance premiums provides yet another incentive for restoring and maintaining good credit.

Coming Up Next

Information you won't find anywhere else: a sample scorecard I obtained from an employee at a credit reporting corporation who asked to remain anonymous. But first, some basic information about how scores are computed that everyone needs to know.

CHAPTER 11

How Credit Scores are Calculated

Credit scores are based on five main types of information:

About 35% based on:	Late payments, collections, judgments, bankruptcies
About 30% based on:	Current debt load
About 15% based on:	How long accounts have been established
About 10% based on:	Type of credit (mortgage, auto loan, hard money loan, etc.)
About 10% based on:	Applications for new credit (credit inquiries)

Factors *not* allowed to be included in your score, per U.S. law, are race, religion, sex, marital status, neighborhood, income, height, weight, or birthplace. This protects Americans against discrimination. This system says that at a given score, applicants of various races, sex, income levels, and so on, are equally likely to pay back their loans as agreed.

The irony is that if these factors were allowed to be considered, then low income groups, certain minority groups, and women would receive higher scores; and thus, it would be easier for them to buy a house. This is because they would be on their own grading curve rather than being thrown in with the population as a whole.

As promised, on the next page is a genuine example of a credit scorecard. To get this, I had to vow not to reveal the name of the employee who gave it to me. Notice the points given for the number of bank cards (credit cards) you have, because this shows you exactly how many credit cards you should have to obtain the maximum amount of credit score points. Also, notice that how old your credit card is affects the number of points you are awarded. This system, which they keep secret from the public, is very interesting and worth studying.

Partial Credit Scorecard

Characteristic	Attributes	Credit Points
Number of bank cards (credit cards)	0	15
	1	22
	2	30
	3	40
	4	30
	5+	20
Number of months in file (How long you've had the account)	< 12 mo.	12
	12 - 23	35
	24 - 47	60
	48+	75
Number of months since most recent bank card opening. (See how opening a new credit hurts your score.)	None	32
	Card but no open date	40
	0 - 5	20
	6 - 11	25
	12 - 17	30
	18 - 23	38
	24 - 35	45
	36+	49
Number of months since most recent derogatory public record. (collections, judgments, bankruptcy, foreclosure)	0 – 5	10
	6 – 11	15
	12 – 23	25
	24 – 47	38
	48+	50
	None	75

CHAPTER 12

Quickest, Easiest Ways to Raise Your Score

If you need to raise your score fast, then start by taking action on the things that *you* control and don't have to depend on getting a creditor's response for. See which and how many of these ten points of wisdom you can implement for yourself.

Ten Tips for Quick Credit Score Improvement

1) Pay down your credit card balances. This is the fastest way to raise your score. As soon as you reduce your balance-to-limit ratio, your score instantly increases. If your balance is over 30 percent of the allowed limit, your score gets docked. If your balance is over 50 percent of the allowed limit, your score gets docked even more. And if your balance is near the limit or maxed out, then you get penalized with a major decrease to your score. The optimal percentage to gain the most points is a balance-to-limit ratio of less than 10 percent. This applies to each individual credit card, and it also applies to the sum of all your credit cards. This is why having more than one card is a good idea, even if you don't personally need more than one. You'll want to use each of your three cards at least once a quarter to keep them active for scoring purposes.

2) If you don't have the cash to pay down your balance immediately, call the credit card company and ask them to raise your limit. This accomplishes the same thing by lowering your ratio. If you have been paying on time, they will usually agree, hoping you'll spend more and owe them more in interest payments. But instead of falling into that trap, don't raise your balance and instead continue to pay down your balance. Your end goal is to pay off the balance in full each time you receive a statement.

3) If you can't get your limit raised and you have a high ratio or are maxed out, you might be able to distribute some of the balance to other existing cards. But whatever you do, you must not open a new card to accomplish this, because as you've seen on the sample scorecard, that would hurt your score for up to 36 months.

4) If you own a business, open a business credit card and then carry your balances on a business card rather than a personal credit card. Only about 10 percent of business cards get reported to the credit bureaus. You can open a business card and move a good portion of your existing balance to that card, which will hide it from the credit bureaus. (Before opening the card, ask if they report to the credit bureaus to get confirmation that they don't.)

5) Use your old credit cards minimally. If you have an inactive card, you are not receiving your "longevity points" for having it. This is important, because 15 percent of your credit score is determined by the age of your accounts. You get more points for maintaining an account for a long time, but if you haven't used your account in several years, it is inactive, and you are missing out on that advantage. Therefore, you should buy something you'd buy anyway, such as milk or a tank of gasoline, at least once every three to four months in order to keep the card in active status for the credit bureaus. (Don't use this as an excuse to buy another pair of shoes or an electronic gadget.)

6) If you have student loans, pay down your balance to below the original amount borrowed (if you have not already done so). This could increase your score by 5 to 10 points.

7) Avoid closing off old credit cards, because doing so could cause your score to go down. This is because with less available credit, your overall debt-to-available credit ratio will be worse.

8) Avoid opening new credit cards if you already have three or more. Whenever you open a new credit card, your score is temporarily penalized, because it is unknown how you will handle the new card.

The exception is if you have only one credit card, no student loans, no auto loans, and no mortgage. If you are young or new to the country and are establishing credit for the first time, you need to obtain a second credit card so you can establish sufficient positive credit. One credit account on your credit report is not sufficient. You cannot qualify for a mortgage or home loan with only one account. You need three trade lines (accounts of some type) on your credit report. At least one of these needs to be a Visa or MasterCard, because these are major cards and have more weight than individual store cards. It is better if you have two major cards and one minor card than the other way around.

9) Set yourself up with automatic pay so that you're never late. For most people, auto-pay is a good idea; that way, you don't take the risk of losing the bill, having the mail get delivered late during inclement weather, or missing a payment while you're traveling, on vacation, or in the hospital.

10) Stay away from finance companies. Before you sign up for financing at an electronic, appliance, or furniture store, ask if they partner with a finance company. If they say yes, do not use their in-store financing. When a finance company shows up on your credit report, it automatically lowers your score—even if you pay on time—because finance companies are considered to be "hard money lenders" who accept people with bad credit. Even if you have perfect credit, having a hard money lender on your report will lower your score. If you already have a finance company on your report, pay if off as fast as you possibly can, especially if the interest rate is high (and it usually is).

CHAPTER 13

How to Get an Awesome Score of 800+

If you want respect from everyone you do business with, if you want your credit score to reflect your good name, if you want your credit to make a statement about your religious faith, then you want that awesome 800 credit score. Don't get me wrong: you can qualify for the best mortgage and auto financing with a 740 score. Nevertheless, there's something about that coveted 800 score!

Achieving a credit score over 800 requires exercising self-control. You can't go wild charging your credit cards to the max, take out finance company loans for your new refrigerator and computer, or get sloppy with payments. You deliberately make the right choices, thereby earning all the applause. No luck is involved. So here's the "Lucky 13."

13 Tips For getting a 800 Score

1. No bankruptcies or foreclosures within the past ten years.

2. No collection, charge-offs, judgments, or liens within the past seven years.

3. No late payments within the past seven years.

4. Mortgage "paid as agreed" with no late payments each and every month.

5. No more than three to five open credit cards. Three is the optimal number.

6. All credit card balances are blow 30% of the limit.

69

7. All installment loans "paid as agreed," with the balance well below the beginning balance.

8. No finance company or other hard money loans on record.

9. Longevity is established; that is, all open accounts are maintained for well over three years.

10. Show stability by having only one or two addresses and only one form of your name listed on your credit report.

11. Establish and maintain emergency funds, savings, and medical insurance as a hedge against unforeseen difficulties so that you do not go late or bankrupt in the future.

12. Do not share your credit cards with anyone except the person you are legally married to. No other family members, not even children, get to use your credit card. No boyfriends, girlfriends, lovers, or engaged partners get to use your credit card. No exceptions. (Feel free to blame your strict policy on this book, if needed. Stand your ground. No one bullies you into using your credit.)

13. Absolutely no co-signing on a loan, credit card, auto financing, or any other financial obligation. Not even for children, parents, a fiancé or fiancée, or Santa Claus himself. You must protect both your credit and debt ratio, and I don't care how trustworthy the person is who is asking for a co-signature, you have only one answer for everyone: NO.

Regarding numbers 12 and 13 above, if after you say no, the person continues to ask, beg, attempt to guilt-trip or cajole you into it, here are some possible responses you can use:

• I'm sorry, but when I say no, it means no. Don't ask me again, because I will not change my mind.

- I don't care if you're the Queen of England, the answer is no.

- My financial advisor will not allow me to participate in a co-signing situation.

- What part of no don't you understand?

- You might not know this, but if I co-sign for you, that obligation goes on my credit report. I am equally responsible for the loan. God forbid, but if you went into a coma, I would be 100 percent legally obligated to pay the entire loan. Furthermore, even if you pay it perfectly all of the time, that obligation goes against my debt ratio. So if I should need to buy a vehicle, get a mortgage, refinance, or make any other financial move, this obligation would block me, because it goes against my debt ratio. So when you understand that, you won't want to put me into a position of co-signing. I'm sure you care about me too much for that.

I've seen good people get denied for home loans, because they didn't know better than to co-sign for their daughter, son, brother, mother, or other dear one. They didn't know it would be counted on their personal debt ratio if the other person was paying the bill faithfully. But it is. Why? Because if that person happened to get run over by a truck or die of an aneurism, you would be 100 percent obligated to the monthly payment.

I've also seen a sickening number of women who had their perfect credit ruined due to co-signing for their sexy man who later quit payment on the loan. The same goes for men who have signed for women, although I haven't seen as many. It seems more men are better at saying no, and it's high time women step up and match them in that regard. Don't let anyone play the "if you love me" card, because that works both ways. If he or she loves you, then they will not put you in that position.

For most people, I think it's simply a matter of educating them. When they ask, they fully intend to make the payments themselves and don't understand that even if they do, it can ruin your debt ratio, block you from making financial moves, and cause your credit score to go down due to overall debt ratios.

Coming Up Next

Now that you have a better understanding of the credit system, it's time to reveal how the pros get late payments deleted from their clients' credit files, and how you can do the same.

CHAPTER 14

Getting Late Payments Deleted Like the Pros

If you want professional results, you need to work like the professionals do. The reason some people think writing a letter to have a late payment deleted doesn't work is because their letters are all wrong. They tell too much and end up verifying their late payment to the creditor, which is exactly the opposite of what they wanted. Or they ask for too much all at once and then wonder why they got denied.

If you dispute all your unwanted items in one letter, you set yourself up for one massive rejection. The credit bureaus will likely label your claim as "frivolous" and toss it out. People who do that then whine, "Credit repair doesn't work." But it does work—when done properly.

If you want professional results, don't write an amateurish letter. Point made. So let's talk about different scenarios and how to handle them, because there is no "one size fits all" letter.

If You Have an Uncharacteristic Late Payment

If you have excellent credit with only one late payment, then that is considered to be an uncharacteristic late. Anyone can read your report and see that you're not the type of person who is chronically late with your payments. There is one blemish, one derogatory late, and that appears to be unusual for you. There are two ways you can handle this situation.

(1) You can dispute the late payment with the credit bureau and point out, "I pay all my creditors on time, as you can see from my report. My credit is very important to me, and I take pride in having

perfect credit. This late payment showing on this account is in error. Please kindly delete it as once, because it is my legal right to have an accurate credit file."

Notice the tone of the letter. It reads like a nice person who expects to be treated nicely in return. I suggest writing a letter like this in longhand to make it even more personal. If your handwriting is legible, it will increase your chances of having the late payment deleted, because it makes you look like the person you say you are: a very nice private person who has just discovered a mistake as opposed to someone who has hired a service to remove a list of derogatory items.

(2) You can write to the creditor that shows the late payment. If you take this approach, whatever you do, you must not admit that you were late! If you do, you could shoot yourself in the foot. The person reading your letter might be one of those legalistic types who has no common sense or no sense of giving grace to good people. So you cannot take that chance.

First, increase your chances of success by taking the time to get the name (and correct spelling) of the individual who handles customer complaints. Don't be lazy and write a Dear Sir or Madam letter, because your letter could get shuffled into the wrong hands and get ignored. Take one shot and aim at the bull's eye. You can find the name of the person to write to on the company website. If you cannot locate it, then do a Google search for:

<company name> + "file a complaint"

By taking the time to locate the proper individual and to write a letter addressed personally to that person, I have had great success with the letters people have hired me to write for them.

Write a letter that says this: "I am a long-standing customer of <company name>, and I have always appreciated the good value and service I have received from <company name.> Recently in reviewing my annual credit report, I was surprised to see a late payment show up. Surely this must be a mistake. As you can see from my payment history, I have a perfect record of paying on time. I would like to remain an active customer of <company name> and will be happy to do so as soon as we get this matter cleared up. Will you kindly send me confirmation that this erroneous late payment has been corrected and deleted from my credit record?"

Insert the name of the company or the store as often as I have it. Companies like to see their own name in print, so spell out the name rather than replace it with a pronoun.

You probably noticed the statement, "I would like to remain an active customer of <company name> and will be happy to do so as soon as we get this matter cleared up." This is a powerful statement. It sounds kind and non-threatening, but it says in no uncertain terms that your business with this company is put on hold until the late payment is gone. The vast majority of companies will respond positively to this request and delete the late payment. And why not? You are a good customer, they want to continue to receive your business, and it is 100 percent legal. Everybody ends up happy.

However, if your letter happens not to receive the normal cooperative response, then you move on to the next step. Don't give up and say it didn't work. You wouldn't expect a professional credit specialist to give up after one try, and neither should you. For your next step, you can request a complete debt validation, which will require them to pull information out of their archives. Or you can take a different approach:, you can bypass the creditor and write to the credit bureau instead. Download the packet of letters to make this as easy as possible for yourself.

If You Have 60-Day and 90-Day Late Payments

If you have a series of late payments, it is highly unlikely that the creditor is going to erase them all in one fell swoop just because you ask. Chances are, they are already more than a little miffed about not getting paid on time as agreed. You have cost them extra money by the loss of revenue and by making them spend time and postage chasing down the payment you owed. So if you write and say, "Hey, will you delete my 90-day late payment?" they are likely to respond with a big, "Forget it!"

So how do the pros get those deep lates off of reports? They do it gradually. "One step at a time" is their secret recipe.

First, they challenge the 90-day late payment without saying anything about the 60-day late or the 30-day late. They contend that you might have been 89 days late, but you were never 90 days late, and that this severe late payment is penalizing your score more than it should. They remind them that The Fair Credit Reporting Act makes it illegal to report false information, so the 90-day mark must be removed.

Then after that success, they challenge the 60-day late payment. And finally, the 30-day late. This is why it takes them more time to clear up credit with deep delinquencies. They don't get a 90-day late payment deleted all at once in 30-days. And the people—including certain authors—who claim to repair all credit *fast* are making false claims. They're baiting you with the promise of *fast* and then switching you to the time-true method later, which is actually dishonest. Personally, I would never work with or recommend a service (or book) that promised fast or quick results, because that is not the reality for most people. Instead of looking for someone who promises *fast*, I would look for an honest professional who promises *persistence*.

This step-by-step, gradual process has been used by professional credit repair services for decades. The law allows consumers to challenge a creditor's records. The law requires transparency. Most companies don't have meticulous records handy, and going back into archives takes time and money. They would rather delete a late payment than pay someone to take the time to prove it.

If a Disaster Caused Your Late Payments

If you were kidnapped at gunpoint and thrown in a cave for 90 days, that could be a sympathetic reason for being late. But even if you could write a story like that, many creditors would still deny your request to delete the late payment. They'll say something like, "We're sorry you were kidnapped, but you should have set up auto-pay to prevent being late." Their thinking is that it's not their fault you were kidnapped, so they shouldn't have to suffer the consequences of not getting paid as agreed.

This is why you shouldn't bother writing about your hospital stay, your fight against cancer, the hurricane that hit your house, the bad divorce, or any other disaster. If you do, you are admitting that you were, in fact, late, which only hurts you even more.

I spoke with a person who said her late payments were due to being a victim of the terrorist attack on 9/11. She wrote a letter explaining this, fully expecting to receive cooperation from the creditor. It didn't work.

Don't count on a creditor having a human heart. Don't ask for sympathy. The approach that works is the approach that says, "I am innocent and you have posted false information, which federal law requires you to correct." That is the approach the professionals use and the approach of the letters included with this book.

Coming Up Next

Clearing up the mystery about how the professionals get the more serious delinquencies removed from people's credit reports.

CHAPTER 15

Deleting Collections and Charge-Offs Like the Pros

If you have a collection or charge-off account on your credit report, this chapter alone is more than worth the price of this book, because it has the potential to save you hundreds, if not thousands, of dollars—*as well as grief, stress, and insomnia.* Science tells us high levels of stress can harm us physically, causing headaches, stomach disorders, and more. Financial stress has been known to cause good, loving relationships to go on the rocks. I would think that is motivation enough.

If you've been searching the Internet for how to take care of collections and charge-offs, you might have come across some false information, because there's a lot of it out there.

Three Misconceptions You Must Not Fall Prey To

Question 1: "If my account was charged-off, does that mean the company got a tax write-off; and therefore, I no longer have to pay the account?"

Answer: No. That would be like saying, "If I steal a leather jacket from Macy's, does that mean they got a tax write-off, so I can keep the coat for free?" Wouldn't it be dandy if that were true! We could all become thieves and help companies lower their taxes at the same time.

If your account is a charge-off, you still owe for the product or service you purchased. It is still going to hurt your credit score until you get it taken care of. I will tell you the best way to do that later in this chapter.

Question 2: "If my unpaid bill is sold to a third-party collection agency, and I never had an agreement with that agency, am I off the hook for the bill?"

Answer: No. That is myth based on only half the truth. Selling unpaid bills to collection agencies is a common practice, and it is legal. You still owe for the product or service you purchased. The collection agency must follow the Fair Debt Collection Practices Act (FDCPA) in order to legally collect from you. You have every legal right to hold them to this before sending any money, as explained in Chapter 2.

Question 3: "If I negotiate for a settlement on my collection or charge-off and end up paying only a fraction of what I owe, will that harm my credit score? Is negotiating a settlement a bad thing to do?"

Answer: Ha, that is a lie some collectors try to feed you! No, negotiating a settlement is not a bad thing. It is a good thing, and you should do it. Getting a settlement and paying less will not make your credit score go down. What's more, don't be intimidated by collectors who try to scare you by saying you'll have to pay taxes on the savings, because that ends up being less money out of your pocket than paying the entire balance. So definitely, go for the settlement. Just make sure you do it like the pros do, as I'll go on to explain.

Take the Proper Steps to Delete Collections Legally

First, get your debt validation, as explained in Chapter 2. If you didn't get it, use the letter template at the end of this chapter to remove the collection off of your credit report. If you are fortunate enough to be successful, you will be rid of the collection without paying any money. If not, skip the letter and read on.

Next and very important, negotiate a settlement that includes a deletion agreement.

Settlements are negotiated every day, but most people don't think about adding a clause that says when the creditor receives the money, the debt will be considered "paid as agreed," and subsequently, they will report to the credit bureaus to delete the collection. This is the BIG SECRET attorneys and certified credit specialists use!

IMPORTANT NOTE The correct verbiage is "paid as agreed." It is not "paid in full," which is inaccurate. If you ask the creditor to write "paid in full," they will say no, because you are settling, not paying in full. "Paid as agreed" is the language the credit bureaus need to see in order to remove the collection. If you paid as agreed, then it means the collection is an error and must be removed.

Is this legal? Yes, it is. The creditor owns your credit information; therefore, they can choose to report it or not to report it to the bureaus. Reporting information to the bureaus is not mandatory.

The Art of Negotiation

Don't be shy about communicating with the creditor. That's all negotiating is, communicating. Some people feel like they hate negotiating, because they envision an ugly, uncomfortable argument, but negotiating like the pros is not that way. I have executed many negotiations for my mortgage clients, and there were never any insults, swearing, yelling, or name calling. I use a professional tone of voice as one professional communicating with another, with the goal of accomplishing an agreement that is acceptable to all parties.

To help you, here is a sample script you can adapt to your own situation:

My name is <state name>. My credit report shows I have a collection with your company, with a balance of $5,000. I'd like to get this taken care of, but I don't have the full $5,000. I can come up with $1,275. If you're willing to settle for that amount, I can send you a cashier's check right away.

Important Strategies

- Don't ever say you need to clean up your credit to buy a car, a house, or to refinance. That will tell them you are anxious, and then they will hold out for more money than they otherwise would. Don't let a shark smell blood!

- Don't be in a rush to pay the creditor. Instead, let them be in a rush to offer you an acceptable settlement so they can get their money.

- Don't believe threats that they will withdraw their settlement offer if you don't pay by a certain date. As one credit repair expert told me, "That's baloney!" They will always want money, and 99 percent of the time, they will make a deal if that's what it takes.

- Always offer a precise odd number, not a round number. It is better to say you can come up with $1,275 than $1,000 or $2,000, because it sounds like you are counting every dollar you've got rather than throwing out some random estimate for them to jack up.

- At this point, don't mention deleting it off your credit report. Not yet. That comes after you have both settled on a pay-off amount.

If the collector replies by saying, "If you settle for less than the whole balance, it will show on your credit report that you settled, and that won't look good."

Then you say, "I already know that, and I am not concerned with it. Will you accept $1,275, or would you rather I pay nothing at all?" (See how that sweeps aside their ridiculous scare tactic and gets back to the issue at hand: the dollar amount of the settlement?)

If the collector replies by saying, "If you settle for less than the entire balance, you will have to pay income tax on that savings."

Then you say, "I already know that, and I am not concerned with it. Will you accept $1,275, or would you rather I pay nothing at all?" (Again, keep on track with the subject: the dollar amount of your settlement.)

IMPORTANT NOTE Don't get into discussions about your credit report or taxes. You lose power when you get into an arguing mode. Your taxes should not be their concern; they're collectors not certified tax accountants. Don't get side-tracked and don't get bullied.

Three Facts You Need to Know

1. It does not affect your credit score one iota if they add verbiage that says you settled. Let them add it. So what! Mortgage and auto finance companies don't care if you settled, so it will not negatively impact your ability to get a car or buy a home. Smart people negotiate a settlement, because they can. Why should you pay more?

2. At the end of the day, you intend to get the collection account completely deleted from your report, so the fact that it is "settled" is a non-issue. However, you must not tell the collector this information, because you're not yet ready to bring it up. Be smart and keep your negotiations professional and amicable. Hold your cards close to your chest, so-to-speak, and don't reveal everything you know or what your future plans are.

3. Even though you may have to declare to the IRS the amount you saved, you still come out far ahead than if you paid your full balance.

It is my strong opinion that you should not agree to pay any of the added interest charges or fees that have driven up your original balance. It is my experience that collection companies will agree to waive the add-ons in order to get paid, if that's what it takes. Keep in mind that they purchased the account for pennies on the dollar, so they are still going to make a profit, even without the fee add-on.

If you offer low, you can expect them to counter-offer. This is fine. The purpose for offering low is to draw out the best offer you can. Sometimes, a person will get lucky, and they will accept your low-ball offer. If not, listen to their counter offer. If it is 50 percent of the balance or lower, then it is a fabulous deal. Here is a sample script:

The collector says, "$1,275 is too low. I can't accept that."

You say, "Well, I'm sorry to hear that, because it's what I've got. What is the absolutely lowest you could offer me?"

The collector then might say, "I can take $2,500, but only if you pay it by the end of the month." (Collectors want payment by the end of the month, because they get paid commissions on a monthly basis.)

So then you say, "I have to tell you, $2,500 is a real stretch. Unfortunately, it is not do-able for me. What if I can manage to get $2,000. Will you take that?"

If they say, "I'll take $2,000 (or any amount) now, and you can pay the rest of the balance next month," DON'T DO IT! Why? Because it is not going to help your credit score to make payments, and it just means a longer paper trail you have to track in order to get it deleted from your credit report. I see no advantage to making payments, especially when it is likely to reset the derogatory account to current and cause your score to go down even more!

So then you say, "No thanks. I want to pay an agreed-upon amount all at once. That is the only way I'm going to do it. One payment, and I'm done. I'll just wait until I can save up for the amount we agree on. If that means I have to wait a year or more, than that's the way it will be." Pause and let that time line soak in. Chances are, the individual won't even be working there a year from now.

Then continue, "On the other hand, if we can agree on a feasible amount, I will pay you this month. Like I said, I want to take care of this, but I am <u>not desperate or in a hurry</u>." (You must always make them believe you are not desperate or in a hurry. Never let a shark smell blood.)

At this point, they might respond by saying, "$2,500 is half off of $5,000. That is the lowest I am authorized to go."

Because 50 percent is an excellent offer, you say, "Please send me a letter saying $2,500 by such-a-date will be **paid in full as agreed.** I'll see what I can do to come up with the funds."

IMPORTANT NOTE You must get this letter! No letter, no payment. No exceptions. I'll explain later, because you are not going to tell your creditor why you want the letter. Simply state that you need a letter saying x amount will be "paid as agreed." Those are the magic words you need. Again, you don't pay a penny until they provide you with a letter confirming your verbal agreement.

Personally, I would be very happy with a 50 percent settlement, but if you want to continue negotiating, that is your prerogative. Some people have more patience and stamina for negotiations than others. The way to get an even lower settlement is to convince them that you neither have the cash nor do you have the ability to get the cash any time in the foreseeable future. A super low settlement takes more time, so you need to consider whether or not the extra time is worth the possible savings. I say possible savings, because every company has their floor for settlements. Not all companies will or can go to 25 percent, for example.

If the creditor offers you 20 percent off with an 80 percent payment, I would hold out. In my experience, all companies will offer 20 percent off, so that is nothing special. They're trying to find your top number, just as you are trying to find their bottom number. Whenever a collector I was speaking to offered me an 80 percent settlement, I responded by saying, "My client doesn't have that much money. If you can't go lower, please consult with your supervisor for an exception. Would you like me to hold on while you check?" I would then hold the line while the collector spoke with (or pretended to speak with) the supervisor, and then he or she would come back with a lower offer.

I probably had a slight advantage as a third party negotiator, because the collector couldn't fault me personally for the bad account. Also, I presented myself as being on their side, trying to help get them money on the account. I said, "Unfortunately, my client has very limited resources." (Feel free to use that expression.) I explained that unless we came up with a do-able sum, there would be no payment at all. I never negotiated payments, only flat pay-off amounts. Once we had a verbal agreement for settlement, I always asked for it in writing as the next step. I had the collector fax me the offer on company letterhead, but an email attachment would be equally acceptable. (I prefer to get the agreement on company letterhead with a signature, not merely an email—and you should follow that protocol as well. Remember, you are now operating as a professional does, not an amateur.)

Present yourself as a calm, rational professional. Do not engage in name calling or yelling. If they call you a name like "Loser" or raise their voice, simply press the "end call" button. An immediate termination to the call will send a message better than anything else.

You must not ever stoop to their level by calling them a name in return, yelling, or swearing. Simply end the call.

Now you have the upper hand. There was money dangling in front of the collector, and he or she has just blown it by acting rudely and therefore causing you to cut off communication. If they call right back, don't pick up. Let them stew for a day. When they call again later, say this: "It is illegal for a creditor to threaten, use obscene language, or harass a debtor. If it happens again, I will promptly report you and your company to the state Attorney General. Now let me speak with your supervisor."

Always maintain control over your voice and your emotions. No screaming, no foul language, and no crying. Don't go into a long, tearful story about your situation. If necessary, put on your "actor's hat" and imitate someone who always keeps their cool, like Victor Newman, James Bond, or your favorite U.S. President.

Once you have negotiated your settlement and have it confirmed in writing, use the following method for paying off the debt. By using this method, you will be able to have the collection removed from your credit report, which is your main goal.

IMPORTANT NOTE Never rely on a verbal agreement for your settlement. Verbal agreements are "forgotten" and "remembered differently." What's more, collectors change jobs frequently, so the individual who made the agreement with you is likely not to be at the firm later. Another collector will then pick up your file and insist you still owe money, even if you paid the amount of the verbal settlement. There is no way you can prove you have paid off the account as agreed unless you have it in writing on company letterhead. One of the worst mistakes people make is handing over money to a collection agency based on a verbal agreement alone.

The ONLY RIGHT WAY to Make Payment on a Collection or Charge-Off

After you have the settlement offer in writing that states $x will be accepted as "paid as agreed," then you can proceed with making payment by check.

Do not pay by cash, because that leaves you without a proper and adequate paper trail, which you might need later.

Never, never, ever give your bank information (not even the name of your bank) to a collector. Do not let them set up automatic withdrawal, because that could result in DISASTER! You should think of the collector as your opponent. You would never let an enemy insert their long, greedy fingers into your bank account, would you? If you divulge your banking information, there is nothing stopping them from automatically drawing out ALL of the money, including their unnecessary late fees and outrageous interest charges as well. You cannot count on what they tell you over the phone in regards as to how much they will withdraw. Verbal promises mean nothing in the world of collections. Verbal promises can be denied later, and then it is your word against theirs, which leaves you as the loser.

As soon as a collector gets your bank account information, he or she will hang up, stand tall in their cubicle, raise their arms and shout, "Woo-hoo! I got one!" Then the manager will emerge from his/her office and give the collector a big high-five and assist in processing the withdrawal. I have been inside collection companies and have witnessed this very thing happen.

Only later do you discover they took out more than what you agreed. You call them up, angry, but it does no good. The collector, now smug, replies, "I never said that. You owe this much, and that's what we took." Click.

What can you do? They've got your money—too much of it—and you were the one who gave them the "key" to open your account.

Pay by check. Refuse to be bullied by threats of not giving you the settlement if you pay by check or money order and don't let them withdraw the money same-day. That's a bunch of boloney. They will be happy to take a check or money order by mail as opposed to receiving nothing at all. If you pay by money order, follow the directions below, the same as if you were paying by check.

Please pay strict attention to the five-step procedure I've outlined here.

Five Mandatory Steps to Getting the Collection Deleted From Your Record

Follow these steps exactly. This is how the best professional credit experts get collections removed from your credit file.

1. When you write your check, on the memo line in the lower left corner, write "paid in full as agreed." If you are using a money order, find a place to write those words on the front.

2. Make four photocopies of your check. One is for you to keep and the other three are for the three credit bureaus. (If only one credit bureau reports the collection, you can make two copies.)

3. Make four copies of your written settlement agreement the collector gave you, same as above.

4. Send in the check to the collector. When they cash the check, they are agreeing to the terms on the front—including the amount and the wording "paid in full as agreed."

5. Keeping one copy for yourself, send in a copy of the check and a copy of your agreement to each credit bureau that reports

the collection. Include a cover letter that says: "This collection must be deleted, because I "paid in full as agreed." By law, you are therefore required to delete this account." This final step is the *secret sauce*, so-to-speak.

IMPORTANT NOTE Up until the point when you write the check, you have been speaking to the collector using the phrase "paid as agreed." But when you actually write your check, expand the phrase to say, "paid in full as agreed."

How to Handle an OLD Collection Account

If your collection account is old and will soon drop off your credit report, then I suggest you ignore it and let it disappear on its own. If no one has contacted you about it, then hopefully, another company won't buy the debt before it drops off your report.

IMPORTANT NOTE If you set up payments or make a partial payment (as opposed to paying in full), you are taking a huge risk, because you might restart the statute of limitations; and thus, make yourself vulnerable to new collection efforts or even a lawsuit for the total balance.

On the other hand, if another collection agency buys the debt, then you will have to deal with it. Sometimes this happens. For example, the state of Rhode Island allows collections to remain on file for ten years, and even if you're not in R.I., many collectors like to set up shop there because of this long time period they have to collect.

Once a collection is seven years old, or has expired according to the appropriate state law, write a letter to the credit bureaus stating how old the account is and demanding that it be taken off your record, per The Fair Credit Reporting Act. The appropriate state is usually the state in which you obtained the loan or the state where you currently live. Sometimes, it is based on the state described in your contract, which is usually the case for credit cards.

When Your Collection Account is Sold to Another Company

A collection agency may sell a debt to another collection company. This happens frequently. However, it is not legal for them to start the seven-year statute of limitations all over again. So, a collection agency can sell a debt that is 15 years old, but they cannot report it to the credit bureaus after seven years from the Date of Last Activity with the original creditor. It is important for you to know this, because some collection agencies violate this law. They continue to report the bad account to the bureaus past the statute of limitations, and unless someone complains, they get away with it.

Duplicate Negative Information Penalize You Twice

You are not supposed to be penalized twice for the same incident, per law. If you were late on your credit card, then the credit card company sold the account to a collector, your credit report might show a 90-day late with the credit card *and* show it with the collector; thus, penalizing your credit score twice for the same account. Letter #12 in the packet of .doc form letters is a dispute letter you send to the credit bureaus to have the duplicate removed. Please note that the duplicate account you want removed is the first, original account with the credit card company (not the latest account with the collector). Because the original creditor sold the account and because it is older, it will be the easiest one to remove. After that success, you can tackle the account with the collection agency: either negotiating a settlement or disputing it, whichever is appropriate for your situation.

Zombie Debts

When a collector sells your old debt to another company and that company continues to report it to the credit bureaus even though it is past the statute of limitations, it is called a zombie debt, because the darn thing keeps raising from the dead and coming back to haunt you.

When writing a letter about a zombie debt, use plain English and demand to have the account removed.

Letters that contain excessive legalese are less successful. If you need to state that you have an attorney who is ready to file a lawsuit, go ahead and state that. It is your legal right to insist that they adhere to the law.

How to Handle Paid Off Collections and Charge-Offs

If you already paid off the collection or charge-off so that it shows a zero balance, you can still get it removed. In Chapter One, I mentioned a loan officer who cleaned up his credit and went on to buy a $975,000 dream home in Woodinville, Washington. Here is the rest of that story.

The loan officer had sufficient income and down payment to buy a house, but his credit score was in the mid-500s. Due to a string of collections from the past when times were tough, he got behind on his bills. However, that was in the past. He had already paid all the delinquent accounts off. But as a result of having those old collections on his report, he couldn't qualify for the loan they needed to buy the house they'd fallen in love with.

I gave Mr. Loan Officer the Credit Investigation Form that is included with this book. Since he had already made good with all the creditors, he did not need to negotiate pay-offs. Therefore, this simple form was sufficient for his situation.

Within just six weeks, a whole page of collections were removed from his credit report, and his credit score rose by 65 points. A few remained, so he went on to step two for those. Since the accounts had remained, his step two was not to ask for credit validation, but rather to dispute again, this time with a written letter, not the Credit Investigation Form he had used previously.

This time, the credit bureaus deleted the remaining paid-off collections off his credit report, permanently. I held the two reports in my hands, side-by-side. Now his score was over 620, and he was qualified for an FHA loan.

One year later, his credit improved even more. Having another 12 months of on-time payments plus the added points of a mortgage loan, boosted his score so that he refinanced into a conventional loan with a lower interest rate. This also confirmed that the removal of those old, paid-off collections was permanent.

If you have zero balance collections, follow Mr. Loan Officer's example. Use the Credit Investigation Form first. Put only one account on the form at a time, unless two accounts are related to one another, such as a duplicate record. I would send up to three forms per week, several days apart. Chances are, each envelope will go to a different representative. Then for the accounts that did not get removed by using the form, send Letter #8 in the packet of letters in .doc form you request from me (see Conclusion). This is the follow up letter to the credit bureau after they deny deleting an old collection. If you need to take step three, send another letter but vary the wording. Read the examples in the packet to get ideas on how to customize your letter.

Be encouraged! An old, paid-off collection will not prevent you from qualifying for a home loan as long as your credit score is at least 620 (FHA). Some lenders will do an FHA loan down to a 580 score at a higher interest rate. If you have good reason to buy a house sooner than later, then take what you qualify for now and make a plan to refinance in a year or two. (Just be sure that you will have the equity to refinance. Do that by purchasing in a neighborhood where values are rising.)

Coming Up Next

If you have a medical collection, the next short chapter contains important information for you.

Sample Letter to Send to the Credit Bureaus After the Collection Agency Fails to Validate Your Debt.

Credit Bureau
PO Box
City, State, Zip code
Date

Re: Account # <fill in number>

Dear Credit Representative:

I am disputing the account stated above. Previously, I disputed this account information with you as being inaccurate; and you responded by stating you were able to verify this debt. But how is this possible? Under the laws of the FDCPA, I have contacted the collection agency myself, and they have failed to verify that this is indeed my debt.

Enclosed are copies of my requests to the collection agency asking them to validate my debt and the receipts showing I sent the letter by certified signature request. In response, I received **no evidence** of my obligation to pay this so-called debt to this collection agency. **This debt does not belong to me, and I am concerned about possible identity theft or fraud.**

The FCRA requires you to verify the validity of this within 30 days. If the validity cannot be confirmed, you are obligated by law to remove it from my credit file.

In the event that you continue to report an unconfirmed, unverified derogatory account on my credit, I will proceed to suing you for actual damages and declaratory relief under the FCRA. According to this regulation, I may sue you in any qualified state or federal court, including small claims court in my area.

I look forward to a swift and amicable resolution to this matter.

Sincerely,
<sign the letter>
Your signature typed

CHAPTER 16

How to Handle Medical Collections

In 2014, the Fair Isaac Company released its updated scoring program called FICO 9. One of the best things about this new scoring model is that it does not penalize consumers with medical collections as severely as it does for other collection accounts. Finally! They have recognized that the circumstances surrounding a delinquent medical bill are not identical to the circumstances surrounding a delinquent credit card.

It is not unusual to discover that an unpaid medical bill is the fault of the insurance company and not the patient. Therefore, it is inaccurate and unfair to penalize the patient's credit score. Additionally, people don't choose to have a medical emergency, so medical bills are not the result of irresponsible over-spending.

FICO 9 differentiates medical from non-medical collection accounts. Medical collections have a lower impact on credit score. By how much? The folks at the Fair Isaac Company say that "the median FICO Score for consumers whose only major negative references are medical collections will increase by 25 points."

Even more encouraging is that the Federal Housing Administration has a new underwriting rule for home buyers who apply for a low-down payment FHA loan. Now, medical collections are not required to be paid off in order to close on a mortgage. That is fantastic news, and it is especially important because as of January 2016, FHA has not yet purchased the new FICO 9. And neither has Fannie Mae.

So what does all this mean for you? If you plan to apply for a credit card or auto loan this year, and you have medical collections on your credit report, you will receive about 25 points of credit grace. This may help you get a better car loan or credit card. However, if you plan to apply for a home loan, then FICO 9 is not going to help you, because the lenders are still using the old FICO scoring model. Therefore, you want to proceed with getting them off your report, as is appropriate per law.

Privacy Laws and Medical Accounts

There is a rumor going around the Internet that says medical delinquencies cannot go on your credit report due to health information privacy laws (HIPAA). This is not entirely true. Medical collections *can* go on your credit report as long as it does not reveal the nature of your illness or issue. For example, it is perfectly legal to post as Northwest Medical Collections. They cannot post as Northwest Cancer Collections or Northwest Weight Loss Solutions, because that would be a violation of privacy.

How to Tackle Medical Bills

First, try to pay at least a minimum payment on your medical bills so that they don't go into collections. Medical bills go into collections faster than other types of debt. What's more, medical offices keep excellent records, so debt validation may not work with medical collection firms. So skip that step and move straight into dispute.

Just because the collection agency is handling medical accounts, it does not mean they are as ethical as your physician. Like all collectors, they might use any tactic at their disposal to collect money. So don't be pressured by threats or bullies. For example, the collector might say, "If you don't pay this bill today, it's going on your credit report." When in fact, it might already be on your credit report.

Seven Strategic Steps For Handling Medical Collections

1. For collections (and charge-offs) that are almost at the seven-year statute of limitations, then you might want to ignore them and let them age off your report naturally. Keep watch so that you write to the bureaus to get them removed if they remain (as sometimes happens) longer than the law dictates.

2. For accurate and affordable collections, pay them off. FICO 9 no longer docks credit points for a paid medical collection. But remember, mortgage companies aren't using FICO 9 yet, so you still need to use the method in Chapter 15 where you write "paid in full as agreed" on the front of your check or money order. Never pay online or with automatic withdrawal, because then you don't have the ability to use this professional strategy.

3. If one medical bill was sold to a collection department, and then that collection department resold it to a different collection company, you could end up with two or three negative collection accounts on your report for one single bill. That is unfair, because you are being penalized more than once for the same thing. It is your legal right to dispute any duplicate medical debt. Use the sample dispute letter at the end of this chapter.

4. Look for inaccurate account numbers. It is not uncommon for account numbers to be reported inaccurately after one company sells its collection files to another. This inaccuracy is a legal loophole you can use to claim "This account is false and not mine. Please delete it at once."

5. According to credit experts, the reason used most successfully for disputing medical collections is stating "wrong person, not my responsibility." If you have a common name, you are especially vulnerable to an identity mix-up. Look up your

name on LinkedIn and Google. For example, there are 103 professionals named Carolyn Warren who use LinkedIn. There are many more than that in the country. If you find another individual's information on your credit report, you have every right to use the Credit Investigation Form and claim "not my account." It also helps if you handwrite a note in the white space that says how many other people have your same name and that you are concerned about identity theft.

6. Disputing a medical collection is like disputing another type of debt. So please refer to the previous chapter for information on how to do that.

7. A paid off medical collection can also be removed by writing a letter that says, "This account never should have gone into collections. It was covered by insurance, was the responsibility of the insurance company, and paid by insurance. Therefore, this is inaccurate and must be removed from my credit immediately."

Final Note About Medical Bills

I am all for taking charge of your credit; however, please do not misunderstand my intentions. We should all pay for the services of physicians, nurses, radiologists, surgeons, and all the other fine, hardworking medical professionals.

If you are successful in getting a duplicate medical collection removed from your report, that is a good thing; and if you get ridiculous late fees and add-ons removed, that is also good. If your insurance company delayed payment and your credit suffers as a result, you should dispute it and get the negative items removed. Do what needs to be done to clean up your credit.

That said, you should still pay for what you honestly do owe. The wonderful folks who devote their careers to caring for us when we are sick or injured deserve to be treated in a fair and honest manner and to be paid for their work.

Coming Up Next

If you have a judgment or lien against you, Chapter 17 tells you how to handle it. If not, you can skip ahead to the next chapter that is applicable to your situation.

Sample Letter to Send to the Credit Bureaus If You Have Duplicate Accounts

Credit Bureau
PO Box
City, State, Zip code
Date

Re: Account # <fill in number>

Dear Credit Representative:

This is a formal complaint about a duplicate collection account appearing on my credit report. This inaccurate reporting is penalizing me unfairly and *illegally*; and this is causing me distress as it is damaging my credit.

Please remove the account stated above immediately. It does not belong on my credit report as it is (1) inaccurate, (2) duplicate, and (3) outdated.

I look forward to a swift and amicable resolution to this matter.

Sincerely,
<sign the letter>
Your signature typed

CHAPTER 17

Deleting Judgments and Liens Like the Pros

If you get served with a false or unfair judgment, rush to the court house and file a Motion to Vacate or a Motion to Dismiss. Doing so is like appealing a verdict that you disagree with. You have the legal right to file such a motion, so do not hesitate.

Whatever you do, you must not ignore a judgment against you, because it will come back to haunt you at the most inconvenient time, like right when you're trying to buy your dream home.

A judgment or lien will not go away just because no one ever contacts you, and then you forget about it. Even if a judgment does not show up on your credit report, if it has been legally filed, it will prevent you from closing on a home loan, because a judgment attaches to your social security number. All mortgage lenders require a title company to do background search for liens and judgments, so they will discover it before closing, even if it's not on your credit report.

I saw this happen to a young, newlywed couple. Right before signing, up popped an old $5,000 judgment attached to the husband's social security number. This was a surprise, because it was not on his credit report. He thought it was "dead and buried," so he never mentioned it to anyone. Now at the eleventh hour, it was blocking them from closing on their home. His wife was not pleased. They did not have the extra five grand, and the attorney office handling the judgment would not budge on the amount. They had to choose between losing the house and their earnest money, or paying off the debt immediately with a credit card. Believe me, it was not a fun scene watching their horror, anger, and frustration. I suppose they were lucky to have a credit card with the available credit, and they did end up getting the house.

This illustrates why it is best to take action as soon as possible.

How to Get a Judgment Overturned

Take the following steps to get a judgment overturned.

1. Fill out the legal document, "Motion and Declaration to Vacate Judgment." You'll see a copy at the end of this chapter. You also receive it in a .doc file with the letter packet, for your ease and convenience.

2. Type out your reasons for bringing the motion. You will need a good reason why you did not respond and appear in court at the time of the hearing for the judgment. Being busy, on vacation, not having a car, or forgetting are *not* good reasons. Here are some acceptable reasons:

- I was not properly served a summons.

- I responded to the summons, but a judgment was issued anyway without a hearing.

- I was unable to answer the summons or appear in court because I was hospitalized.

- I was unable to answer the summons or appear in court because I was out of the country, serving in the military.

- The collection agency failed to respond to my request for validation; therefore, they failed to provide proof that the debt was my responsibility, under the Federal Debt Collection Protection Act (FDCPA).

Caution: Do not write an excuse such as, "My ex was supposed to pay this," or "My insurance company was supposed to handle this." Those reasons are not acceptable and will not work, because they show negligence on your part for not showing up in court to explain that at the hearing. The court responds only to violations of existing laws.

3. File the paperwork.

Normally, you file your Motion and Declaration to Vacate in the same court that granted the original judgment. However, you may be able to handle it by mail if you have moved away. Call the original court to find out if this is possible for your situation. The clerk at the court can help you with the paperwork required for your particular state.

The court will set a date for the hearing, usually about 35 days from the time you file.

4. Notify the Plaintiff, if needed. (The person who filed the judgment against you.) When you file the documentation, ask the clerk if you need to notify the Plaintiff or if the court will do that. If it is your responsibility, the clerk will also give you acceptable options for notification in your state, such as using a professional server or using certified mail.

If The Plaintiff Offers to Settle

Oftentimes, the Plaintiff will offer to settle the issue outside of court, especially if they are in the wrong or if they have no proof of their claim. If this happens, follow *all* of these four steps:

1. Demand that they file paperwork to dismiss the lawsuit.

2. Demand that they notify any collection agencies that were involved.

3. Demand that they notify each credit bureau and provide you with a copy of the letter sent to the credit bureaus. (This letter is like gold to you! Keep it in a secure place, such as a fireproof safe or a bank safe deposit box.)

4. Make sure you receive a copy of the documentation from the court that states your judgment was vacated or dismissed *before you sign an agreement to settle.*

If You Go to Court

If you are lucky, the Plaintiff will not show up for the court hearing, and you will therefore win by default.

If the Plaintiff shows up but fails to provide proper documentation that proves you were properly served, that the amount of the debt was correct, and that you are responsible for the debt, you will win.

After winning, follow up with the credit bureaus by sending them copies (always keep your originals!) of the judgment dismissal. This will significantly improve your credit score the moment they remove it from your credit file, which could take up to 30 days.

If you lose, try to work out a reasonable payment plan, and hopefully, a reduced payment amount. The Plaintiff might be willing to accept less than the full amount if you convince them it is all you have and that you will pay immediately in full—for, say, 60 percent of the balance. Start with 60 percent, 40 percent off. If they agree to a 20 percent reduction or better, I suggest taking it. Again, make sure you get the settlement agreement in writing first, so you don't get scammed later. (If you didn't read about that in Chapter 15, this is a good time to go back and read that important information.)

When You Owe the Judgment or Lien

If you do owe money to the Plaintiff, take care of it as quickly as you can so you can put it behind you and get on with your business. Try to work out a settlement that excludes late fees and interest charges. Or, you might set up a payment plan; but in that case, you won't receive as low cash settlement, and it will drag on longer.

A judgment or lien is not a permanent situation, so take heart. People make mistakes and recover. Losing money is a minor setback, not a disaster. It happens to a lot of good people. Life goes on.

Coming Up Next

If you had a bankruptcy or if you're curious about the topic of bankruptcy, the next chapter is for you. If not, you might choose to skip ahead.

Sample Motion to Vacate

IN THE SUPERIOR COURT OF THE STATE OF <YOUR STATE>

IN AND FOR THE COUNTY OF <YOUR COUNTY>

<The Original Plaintiff's name> Plaintiff,

vs.

<Your name>, Defendant

No. <COURT REFERENCE NUMBER>

MOTION AND DECLARATION TO VACATE JUDGMENT

NOW COMES the Plaintiff, Pro Se and prays this Honorable Court to Deny the Defendant's Motion to Dismiss and Motion for Sanction for the following reasons:

1. Relief requested. The defendant(s) move(s) the court for an order vacating the judgment entered in this action and staying enforcement of the writ of restitution until the motion can be heard.

2. Statement of facts and issues. This motion is based on the following grounds: <Enter your reasons: you were not properly served, the judgment was entered even though you filed the correct paperwork, or as applicable.>

Dated: _____

_____
Defendant signature

Defendant name printed
Address
Telephone number

DECLARATION

I, <name>, declare as follows:

1. I am the defendant in this unlawful detainer action.

2. I request that the judgment entered in this action be vacated for the following reason: <State your reason per suggestions above.>

I certify under penalty of perjury under the laws of the state of <YOUR STATE> that the foregoing statement is true.

Signed in <CITY>, <STATE> on <DATE>.

_____
Signature

<Name, printed or typed>

CHAPTER 18

Dealing with a Bankruptcy

If you had a bankruptcy in the past, don't despair. Many successful people chose to declare bankruptcy because it was the best financial move for them at the time. These people don't stay down in the dumps; they bounce back to be better than ever. Here are some examples.

- Henry Ford declared bankruptcy soon after he started his first automobile business. The second time he started a business, it was a success, and Ford became a leader in the auto industry.

- Walt Disney went bankrupt in 1923 after his first film studio went bust. Then in 1928, he unveiled a new cartoon character named Mickey Mouse, the first of many successes to follow.

- Abraham Lincoln fell into bankruptcy as a young man after he purchased a shop that failed. He lost many of his personal possessions, including his horse. But he went on to become one of history's most celebrated, wise, and successful Presidents.

- Cyndi Lauper declared bankruptcy after her first attempt to get into the music business. Then in the mid-1980s, she became the first female singer to have four top-five singles released from one album. As of 2008, she sold more than 25 million records worldwide.

- Donald Trump, according to *Forbes*, filed for corporate bankruptcy in 1991, 1992, 2004, and 2009. He hasn't let this stop him from going on to success, and I highly doubt it hurt his self-esteem either. In 2015, The Donald declared that he was worth $10 billion. If you think that figure is exaggerated and cut it in half, it is still a lot of money.

If your Chapter 7 bankruptcy was discharged more than ten years ago, or if your Chapter 13 bankruptcy was discharged more than seven years ago, it should have dropped off your credit report. If that didn't happen, write a letter to the credit bureau(s) that still show the BK stating that the time for reporting it has expired and therefore, it needs to be removed. It should come off, pronto. (BK is the abbreviation used in the mortgage industry for bankruptcy.)

On the other hand, if your BK has not reached the bureaus' expiration date, then you can take steps to try to get it removed, as the pros do.

Don't Admit Guilt

Whatever you do, *don't* send a letter that says, "You have my discharge date and the case number wrong, so delete the bankruptcy." If you do, you have just admitted that you did indeed declare bankruptcy and that you know the correct date and case number. Then the credit bureau will research the info, correct it, and make sure your BK sticks on record.

Set Yourself Up for Success

Your first step is to go to www.optoutprescreen.com and opt out of the information sharing system. Do not neglect this important first step.

Second, if possible, get the address under which you filed bankruptcy deleted from your report. This is a key step to success, so if you can do this, you'll have a better chance. However, if you are still living at the address you used when you filed BK, or if you have current accounts tied to the same address as your BK, then you won't be able to get that address off your report. In that case, you will use a different approach.

This is where two approaches, a veritable fork in the road, emerge. Choose the path according to your situation and comfort level.

Approach #1: If You Can Remove the Address Tied to the Bankruptcy

Here is the true story of how one man who is calling himself "Robert Smith" was successful in getting the Chapter 7 BK deleted off his report. As of now, and it has been over four years, it has not reappeared on his report, so it looks like permanent success.

After opting out and having the address removed, his third step was to send a letter disputing the public record (bankruptcy) as "someone with a similar name." Not only is his name common, but when he was in school, there was another student with the same name and birthdate as his. Now that he's an adult, this is a loophole he uses to his advantage.

Upon first request, Equifax deleted the bankruptcy. TransUnion and Experian did not. So he continued his work.

Pursuant to Rule 1005 of the Federal Rules of Bankruptcy Procedure, all documents filed with the court are to contain only the last four digits of an individual's social security number or tax identification number.

Robert then filed a motion to seal all documents that were filed with the court. Under the Federal rules of Bankruptcy Procedure, a debtor's full social security number is filed with the original petition and filed under seal. This means the only information released to third parties who are not directly involved in the case is your full name, your address, and the last four digits of your social security number.

Robert sent a letter to the Clerk of his local court in the Eastern District of Virginia. It, along with the clerk's reply, is very interesting. Here it is:

Dear Clerk,

My name is Robert Smith, and I am writing you because an entry appears on my credit report which states that I filed bankruptcy in your district. Could you please explain to me how this might occur? From my understanding, only the last four digits of a debtor's social security number are released to third parties, pursuant to the Federal Rules of Bankruptcy Procedure. Any information you can provide me would be appreciated.

Sincerely,
Robert Smith

The reply letter from the Clerk was as follows:

Mr. Smith,

The United States Bankruptcy Court for the Eastern District of Virginia does not provide any information to any credit bureaus, all information they obtain is via third party. You are correct that pursuant both to Federal Statute and the Federal Rules of Bankruptcy Procedure only the last four digits of a Debtor's social security number along with their full name and address can be released. In order to obtain a debtor's full social security number, a third party must file a motion with the court to unseal documents related to a case. This would be very unusual and does not happen on a regular basis. I hope this letter is helpful in your matter.

Sincerely,
Clerk of Court

Armed with this information, Robert wrote to TransUnion's and Experian's executive office staff. Remember, the address associated with his bankruptcy was no longer on his report. Here is what his letter said:

Dear Mr. <Executive's name>

My name is Robert Smith and I am writing you about an entry listed on my credit report which I have tried to have removed. Apparently someone with a similar name to mine filed bankruptcy in the Eastern District of Virginia, and it appeared on my credit report. Through your dispute system I recently filed a dispute stating that someone with a similar name had filed this public record, and it was not mine. Unfortunately, it came back verified and it is still listed on my credit report. Frustrated, I decided to contact the Bankruptcy Court, and they informed me that they do not provide anyone with a debtor's full social security number; and they do not provide any credit bureau any information relating to any bankruptcy cases. As you well know, it is a violation of the Fair Credit Reporting Act to report erroneous information on a credit report. I ask that you remove it immediately.

Sincerely,
Robert Smith

As a result, he received prompt replies from both Experian and TransUnion. Please note that he addressed the letters to the specific individuals, taking care to look up the correct spelling of their names. Both bureaus deleted the bankruptcy off his credit report.

Subsequently, he was able to dispute all the accounts that said "included in bankruptcy," (I.I.B.) because the bankruptcy itself was now gone. Several weeks later, all of the I.I.B. accounts were also deleted. Please note that he first made sure that the old address tied to the I.I.B. accounts had been removed.

Robert said he saw "quite a nice jump" in his credit scores and was able to proceed to refinance his auto loan into a lower rate and payment as well as lower the rates on his credit cards.

The basis for his arguments was that without full social security numbers, the creditors could not tie the bad public record and bad accounts to him. He was also careful in his letter to the Clerk of Court not to state anything that was false. You might want to go back and read it again. Be careful that you do not lie or commit fraud to a court of law.

Even though Robert Smith had the bankruptcy removed from his credit report, it does not necessarily mean it is no longer tied to his actual social security number. If he were to apply for a mortgage, the bank or lender would have the title company do a search, which is likely to reveal the bankruptcy.

The bottom line is that by having the BK and other baddies removed, Robert raises his credit score and saves money on consumer loans. But to buy a house, he will need to wait the 24 months required by FHA. (Conventional loans take longer.) Having a higher credit score will help him qualify for a better interest rate on his mortgage and a lower premium on his insurance.

Approach #2

A professional credit restoration service that has helped over 20,000 clients uses a different approach, which tackles the problem from the opposite angle. Before sending a letter requesting a bankruptcy to be removed, they say to first take these necessary steps:

1. Opt out at www.optoutprescreen.com.

2. Read through your credit report and find all the individual accounts that say "included in bankruptcy." One by one, get those accounts deleted by sending a letter that says the account was not yours and therefore must be deleted from your records.

3. Find the addresses of your past residences on your credit report. Send a letter disputing the address you were at when you filed BK. You don't want the bankruptcy to be linked to you through the address. This is an essential but often-overlooked step!

4. 4) Wait one month after you have the information in #1 and #2 above cleared off your report, then send a letter to the credit bureau that says, "I have no public record with the details you are reporting. It appears you have mixed up somebody else with me and have reported their ugly credit on my report. Please delete this bankruptcy from my credit file immediately."

That doesn't sound like a legal form letter, does it? It doesn't sound like it came from a lawyer or a credit repair company, either. That is precisely why it works. It would be a good idea to modify the wording somewhat more in order to fit your own personality; as long as you don't make it sound like it's a copied form letter. But remember, no foul language; that would only make them angry and dig in their heels. By sending a personal letter of dispute, it increases your chances of success in having the bankruptcy deleted.

A Surprising Success Strategy You Can Use

A husband and wife sent out letters of dispute to the credit bureaus regarding their bankruptcy. The husband sent a neatly handwritten letter on lined, legal-sized yellow paper. The wife had hers typed and printed out on white paper. Guess who got their bankruptcy deleted and who got a letter back saying the bankruptcy was verified and would remain on record...?

The husband's yellow handwritten letter was successful, and the wife's computer-printed letter was not. This illustrates why I advise personalizing your letter just a bit.

Approach #3: Stir Up Confusion to Gain Success

Another credit repair guru claims he has a clever strategy that works for removing bankruptcies. It's about stirring up confusion. I have not seen it tried, and I do not advocate doing it. But as a point of interest as to how some professionals work, here it is.

The credit specialist says to first wait 27 months after the discharge date. Why? Because bankruptcy courts keep cases active for 24 months, and then send the files to the archives.

Then send a dispute letter stating your bankruptcy is the opposite of what it was. You say your bankruptcy was a Chapter 13, not a Chapter 7. Or, send a dispute stating your bankruptcy was a Chapter 7, not a Chapter 13. (Whichever is opposite of what it says on the credit report.) No need to send any supporting documentation, just the letter.

According to this particular credit pro, bankruptcy courts do not respond to requests for verification on cases that have already been archived; therefore, they delete the bankruptcy, and it disappears permanently.

"The worst bankruptcy in the world is the man who has lost his enthusiasm. Let a man lose everything else in the world but his enthusiasm, and he will come through again to success."

~ H.W. Arnold

Speaking of enthusiasm, here is the terse letter one young gentleman sent to the credit reporting agencies.

Dear CRA:

(1) Please remove the bankruptcy notation on my credit report.

(2) I have only been bankrupt once, while playing Monopoly with my cousin Hank.

(3) I think he cheated. I don't remember him ever buying North Caroline Avenue, but after I got back from getting the nachos, he suddenly had the card.

So even that bankruptcy doesn't count.

(5) I PWNed him the next time we played!! LOL!!!!

No word on whether or not this letter worked, but it was funny.

CHAPTER 19

Handling a Foreclosure Like the Pros

"Men's best successes come after their disappointments," said Henry Ward Beecher, minister and lecturer. If you suffered the disappointment of a foreclosure, remember this: it is not the end of your story. You have the ability to rebuild your credit and own property again.

I lost a dream home myself—not due to foreclosure, but due to a crazy divorce—so I know how it feels to go from living in a spacious house in an upscale neighborhood to a tiny rental apartment just blocks from a bad highway. I know what it feels like to move the children across town from one school to another. In those days, I was one of the working poor. A full-time job didn't pay enough for survival, so I qualified for food stamps. And now, I'd like to tell you a secret about how I survived those hard times and moved on to better.

It never occurred to me that I was in poverty or poor. I thought I was going through a temporary hard time. The key word being *temporary*. I've found that one of the greatest secrets to success in life is your mindset. "As a man thinks in his heart, so is he." (Proverbs 23:7) If you think you're doomed, you will be. If you think better days are ahead, you have hope, and you will move into better times. Since you're reading this book, it shows that you, too, have hope, and I commend you for that.

The point I want to make is that a foreclosure is not the end of the line for you. A dental hygienist told me his brother was planning his suicide because he felt like he couldn't face the humiliation of a foreclosure. Fortunately, the family learned of his plan and intervened.

How tragic if his story had ended at his black moment!

Americans love a good comeback. Think about all the celebrities and sports heroes who have messed up royally—and have had their disasters published all over the tabloids. And then think about all the ones who made their comeback and rose to even more popularity, fame, and fortune. If you had a foreclosure, pick yourself up and stage your own personal comeback.

With that word of encouragement, here is how the credit repair experts succeed in having foreclosures removed from the credit reports of their clients:

1) Wait a minimum of 24 months after the sale has been completed on the property. Note that this is not 24 months after your notice of foreclosure. You must wait until the sale has been finalized and then add two more years.

2) Send a dispute letter to the credit bureaus stating the foreclosure on your record is inaccurate and you demand a copy of the records for your review, which is your legal right per law.

Since the paperwork is archived, it will be nearly impossible and certainly impractical to produce it. Therefore, the disputed derogatory item, namely the foreclosure, must be deleted. Again, it's "innocent until proven guilty."

I was privy to a seminar by and for professionals on credit improvement. The expert-speaker said that in a foreclosure, the dates are often wrong. The bank might file paperwork six months after the foreclosure took place. If your dates are incorrect, you have every right to send a letter stating, "I did not have a foreclosure on month/day/year. Please remove this error at once."

Be prepared to send multiple dispute letters. The first time they respond with a snappy letter saying sorry, the foreclosure stands, does not mean that they did a proper job of researching it. This is one of the dirtiest secrets of the credit bureaus. Oftentimes, they send back "verification letters," when not one iota of research or verification has been done. So if that happens, don't be surprised. Simply fire off your second dispute letters, again demanding a copy of the records for your review, per law.

As the credit repair specialists will tell you, having a foreclosure removed takes time, persistence, tenacity, and patience. It is no small thing; nevertheless, it is done.

If, after repeated attempts, you don't find success, wait six to twelve months, and then try again. However, even if you don't achieve success in getting the foreclosure deleted, remember that you can become a property owner again in one of three ways: (1) by waiting out the time required, (2) by working out private owner financing, or (3) by paying cash.

Coming Up Next

A little known secret (that the credit bureaus try to deny) is in the next chapter. This is a fine tuning step you can use after the major credit work is done. Think of it like the cherry on top of the sundae.

CHAPTER 20

Removing Extra Names and Addresses From Your Report

I first learned this tip from Correct Credit Company, Inc., which has helped more than 20,000 people legally improve their credit. More recently, it has been confirmed by Approval Guard, a credit monitoring service used by one of the major credit bureaus; and by Chad Kusner, Board Member of the National Association of Credit Services Organizations.

Ideally, you want to have all of your accounts and financial dealings under one form of your name. If you are a Sr., Jr., or Third, you want the surname included also in order to separate your credit from the other individuals with similar names. Not only will this eliminate confusion, but it has been shown to raise credit scores by 5 to 20 points when the extra names come off the report.

It appears that the credit bureaus don't want the public to know this secret, because they claim it makes no difference. However, the experience of the top credit repair specialists says otherwise! They confirm that their clients' scores do improve when superfluous names and addresses are removed. Why? Because the perception of stability increases with one name and longstanding addresses. Stable people pay their bills, so that's what they want to see. We all know a person can be stable and still move a lot, and this is probably why the bureaus deny that it helps. Nevertheless, those who do thousands of credit improvements over decades of time say it does matter.

By way of example, if your name is Patricia Mary Scott and you changed your name after marriage to Patricia Mary Patterson, you don't want your credit report to look like this:

Patricia Scott
Patty Scott
Patricia M. Scott
Patricia Patterson
Pat Patterson
Pat M. Patterson
Patricia Mary Patterson
Patricia M. Patterson
P. M. Patterson

That adds up to nine names for one woman! If she has good credit and a score of 790, and she gets all the names deleted except for Patricia M. Scott and Patricia M. Patterson, her score is likely to top 800, which is something to brag about!

However, here is the problem, one you're likely to run into for yourself. Let's say she sends a letter stating, "Patricia M. Patterson is my only correct and true name, so please delete all others." But then on her credit report, there is an old auto loan that was financed under the name of Patricia Scott. In addition, she has a credit card with the name Pat Patterson. The credit bureaus will not delete those two names, because they are anchored with an established credit history.

In situations like this, you must dispute the old, paid-off auto loan as belonging to you as well as the alternate name. In addition, you need to contact your credit card company and have them correct your name on the credit card to the one, correct form of your name. After giving them 45 days to update the records, send a Notice of Correction to the credit bureaus.

At the end of this chapter, there is a form letter you can use for deleting incorrect names. It is a good idea to include a copy of your driver's license and security card for verification.

Too Many Addresses?

If you happen to have an extraordinarily large number of addresses on your report, then you should consider having some of those deleted, too. Look for addresses of places where you have never lived. Look for your parents' address. In addition, if there are addresses where you have no credit tied, you can remove those as well.

It is normal for a person to move, so having a few addresses on your report is normal and just fine. The addresses of previous mortgages you have had will be on your credit report, and you want to retain those, because a mortgage that has been paid on time is an asset to a credit report. On the other hand, if you have 15 addresses and five of them are places you lived at for a year or less with no credit tied, I recommend sending a letter asking for those to be removed.

Following are two letters you can use to have superfluous names deleted. Choose the one that best fits your situation. Then following those is a letter you can use to have incorrect addresses deleted.

Coming Up Next

Even though inquiries are not a major factor in credit scoring, they do count. The next chapter explains what every citizen needs to know about credit inquiries.

Sample Letter to the Credit Bureau For Incorrect Names to Be Removed

Your name
Your address
City, State, Zip code
Credit Bureau
PO Box
City, State, Zip code

Date

Dear Credit Representative:

I have recently reviewed my credit report, and I noticed that you have reported an incorrect name on my report, as follows:

Incorrect Name
<State name in error.>
Correct Name
<State correct name.>

With the amount of identity theft happening now, I am concerned that someone could mistakenly identify me as someone else, even a person with a similar name to mine. Therefore, I am asking you to correct this information by removing the incorrect name and leaving only my correct name on my file, as stated above.

In addition, please delete any accounts that are attached to the person whose name is similar to mine, as stated above under "Incorrect name."

Sincerely,
<Sign the letter>
Type your signature here

Sample Letter to a Creditor to Have Someone Else's Account Removed

Your name
Your address
City, State, Zip code

Creditor
Address
City, State, Zip code

Date:

Dear Credit Representative:

I recently obtained a copy of my credit report and discovered that it contains inaccurate information that was provided by your company.

The accounts listed below do not belong to me; and therefore, they should not appear on my credit report. In this day and age when identify theft and impersonation is the fastest growing crime in the U.S., I am concerned about this account with a name similar to mine showing up on my credit report. Please remove both the account and the name, <fill in wrong name here>, from my credit file immediately.

<credit account name, account #>

<credit account name, account #>

I would like to remind you that failing to accurately report information on my credit report is a violation of the [15 U.S.C. § 1681s-2](a) (1) (A) *Reporting information with actual knowledge of errors.*

When you have corrected the inaccurate information described above, please send a corrected report to me. I expect you to comply without delay or further argument. If not, I will be forced to pursue legal action, as I cannot and will not tolerate someone else's account and name showing up on my credit report. You should also know that neither TransUnion nor Equifax reports the above, so the error is solely with your company. <Add last sentence only if true. Edit as needed.>

Sincerely,
<Sign your letter>
Type your signature

Sample Letter to Have Incorrect Addresses Removed

Your Name
Address
City, State, Zip code
Birth date
Social Security #

Credit Bureau
Credit Bureau Address
City, State, Zip code

Date

Dear Credit Bureau Representative:

I have recently reviewed my credit report, and I noticed you have reported an incorrect address on my report, as follows:

Incorrect Address

<State address in error.>

Correct Addresses

<Address>
<Address>
<Address>

With the amount of identity theft happening now, I am concerned that someone could mistakenly identify me as someone else due to an incorrect address appearing on my report. Therefore, I am asking you to correct this information by removing the incorrect address and including only the correct ones, as stated above.

Sincerely,
<Sign your letter>
Type your signature

CHAPTER 21

Delete Inquiries Like the Pros

If you have already seen your credit report, you may have noticed a list of creditors that have made what is called an inquiry about your credit.

"Hey, what's going on here?" you might ask. "I never gave permission to Visa or American Express or Chevron to pull my credit report! I wonder how much this has docked my score?"

Before you get upset, you need to know there are two kinds of credit inquiries. One does not affect your score whatsoever, so there is no cause for concern. The other does affect your score, and in a moment, I will tell you how to get rid of that pesky inquiry.

Soft Inquiries

A soft inquiry is when a credit card company or your current mortgage lender reviews your credit file to see if there are any recent late payments. This is an automatic inquiry that is conducted by their computer software. It scans millions of credit files. It is not an individual person reading through your report—they don't have time for that.

Additionally, credit card companies scour credit files in search of new suckers, er, potential customers. They might look for everyone who has a score over 700 in certain zip codes, for example; and then they send those people a solicitation letter for a credit card. You have probably received those annoying offers. These inquiries do not affect your score in any way.

Your current credit card company and your current mortgage company may also review your credit file for late payments. They are protecting their own interests when they check to see if it looks like you're getting into financial trouble. If you paid late on your Providian credit card, then Visa is likely to raise your interest rate on their card, even though you were never late with it. This is because they think you are getting into trouble and might be late with them next.

Suddenly, they see you as a high risk borrower, and they might jack up your interest rate to some outrageous amount, like 22% or 32%. Yes, it is legal. All they have to do is notify you in tiny print first, so it's a good idea to pay attention to letters from your creditors.

A mortgage company cannot raise your interest when you get behind on your credit cards, because you have a set mortgage contract: the Loan Note. But they may still look, because if you are getting behind on your financial obligations, they may want to call and offer you a refinance to pay off your credit cards. Of course, this is *not* in your best interest the majority of the time, because a larger loan eats up your precious home equity.

Hard Inquiries

If you ever clicked on an Internet ad for a mortgage, this information is for you. The ads can be quite deceptive. It might beckon you with an innocent piece of intelligence, such as, "Find out what rates are in your area." It sucks you in by asking you to fill in your zip code. Nothing too personal, right? That leads to other questions, and by the end, you're giving out very personal information such as your social security number—and of course, your email address in order to receive the information. Somewhere in there is fine print that gives them permission to pull your credit report. Why else would they need your social security number if not for pulling your credit? This is called a hard credit inquiry, as opposed to a soft inquiry.

A hard inquiry is when you apply for credit—either for a credit card, auto financing, a mortgage, or a consumer loan—and the company pulls your credit report with your authorization. If any company conducts a hard inquiry, it *might* affect your credit score; therefore, they do not have the legal right to do this without first receiving your authorization.

If a company pulled your credit without your permission, you have the right to have that inquiry removed from your report. If you clicked on a mortgage ad and entered your social security number, but did not read the fine print or understand that your credit report would be pulled, then you can still request that the inquiry be removed. Yes, it is your fault for not reading the fine print; and no, you cannot sue the company. Nevertheless, you can send a letter stating you did not give permission (because you did not do so with understanding) and demand the inquiry be deleted.

One gentleman wrote to tell me that he clicked on an ad for LendingTree while he was passing the time in a hospital waiting room. Next thing he knew, he was inundated with emails and phone calls from mortgage lenders. "Boy, did I ever feel silly," he said.

Although the bureaus are not technically required to delete the inquiry in a case of the consumer's neglect to read the fine print, you can still send the letter, and why not?

At the end of this chapter is a form letter you can use to request this type of hard inquiry deleted. But please, don't bother sending it for soft inquiries, because you will be wasting your time and postage. Remember, the soft inquiries are simply computer programs scanning for certain information, and they do *not* affect your score in any way.

How Much Do Inquiries Affect Your Credit Score?

Many people are concerned about inquiries to their credit reports, as well as whether or not inquiries will cause them to be disqualified for a good home loan. It only takes one or two published stories to start rumors spreading like wildfire. Some feature reporters (who are not in the lending or credit business) have grabbed onto some quotes and written up a "big scare." "Big scares make big stories, but when you put the scary information into proper context, you might find the fright is a lot more bark than bite.

Some loan officers have said to their potential clients, "Don't shop with any other mortgage company, because inquiries on your credit report will lower your score, and then you won't be able to get a good loan." It makes a person wonder if they are afraid of the competition!

Let me assure you that it is not the intention of the credit bureaus to deny consumers the right to shop for a loan. There is no need to panic about inquiries. Here are the facts:

- An inquiry can cost a consumer from 2 to 50 points, with an average being 3 to 35 points, *when inquiries are a factor*.

- Employer-Employee inquiries are not counted in the score.

- A request you make to obtain your annual free credit report does not count as an inquiry.

- The credit bureaus say that you can have as many mortgage inquiries and auto finance inquiries as you like within a 30-day period, and it will count as only one inquiry on your scoring model.

- A 30-day buffer for mortgage and auto inquiries protects you from having your score docked while you shop for the best loan. Nevertheless, you do not want to have more than three mortgage inquiries, in my opinion. Too many mortgage inquiries sets off a red flag alert to mortgage underwriters, because they think other lenders are rejecting your applications. How many is too many? One underwriter told me six sets off a red flag.

- Mortgage (or auto) inquiries that are spread out beyond the 30-day grace period will affect credit scoring, if the inquiries are older than 30 days from the date your credit report is pulled.

- Inquiries affect credit scores the least of all the factors, only 10%. For most people, this small effect would not be a concern. For those with scores on the border, it is something to be aware of.

- Multiple credit card inquiries will negatively impact credit scores. This is because it is very plausible that you could take out five or six credit cards at once and then dramatically increase your debt, and thus your credit risk. You should avoid opening new credit card accounts if you already have three or four open.

- You have the right to stop solicitations for credit cards. I highly recommend this! Use either the automated telephone system at 1-888-567-8688 or go to www.optoutprescreen.com. The online source is secure and safe.

- Applying for credit can equate to being a higher credit risk. This is important, and not many people know this. When you plan to buy a house, avoid opening a new credit card. Do not apply for an auto loan. For the six months prior to getting a mortgage, do not apply for any new credit—not even for a discount on your clothing purchase. It is not worth it to have points subtracted from your score due to creditor inquiries.

Illegal Credit Inquiries

The Fair Credit Reporting Act states that there are only four permissible purposes for pulling an individual's credit report:

1) A firm offer of credit.

2) Insurance.

133

3) An application for employment.

4) A court order.

Following is a form letter you can use to have unauthorized inquiries deleted from your credit report. This is the type of letter used by professional credit restoration services.

Coming Up Next

A specific plan and checklist for success is in the next chapter. You're almost done, so please read on.

Sample Letter for Having Unauthorized Credit Inquiries Deleted

Your Name
Address
City, State, Zip code
Birth date
Social Security #

Credit Bureau
Credit Bureau Address
City, State, Zip code

Date:

Dear Credit Bureau Representative:

I recently reviewed a copy of my credit report and noticed the following information regarding inquiries to be in error. The Fair Credit Reporting Act states that the only permissible purpose for pulling a person's credit report is 91) a firm offer of credit, (2) insurance, (3) an application for employment, or (4) a court order.

The following inquiries are not related to one of the allowable purposes, as I have reiterated from The Fair Credit Reporting Act.

1. <name of company with unauthorized inquiry>
2. <name of company with unauthorized inquiry>
3. <name of company with unauthorized inquiry>
4. <name of company with unauthorized inquiry>
5. <name of company with unauthorized inquiry>

Please remove these inquiries from my credit report immediately.
Thank you.

Sincerely,
<Sign your letter>
Type your signature here

135

CHAPTER 22

Build Great Credit and Achieve a High Score

After you get rid of the negative information on your credit report, you are going to need to show positive credit. You cannot achieve a high credit score without positive credit, neither can you get approved for a home loan without positive credit. Accordingly, here are directions for taking this next important step.

I recommend copying out the list below the old fashioned way, with pen and paper. The act of writing it out will help cement it in your memory. But if you prefer, creating a Word document is also effective.

After your list is written, write a nice, big X on the numbers of the items you are already doing. Circle the numbers of the items you need to do, and get to work on those.

Review the list at least once a month. Put it on your calendar so you don't forget. When a circled item is completed, X it out. There is a lot of satisfaction from seeing your progress with the big Xs.

MY ESSENTIAL LIST FOR CREDIT SUCCESS

1. Establish credit in my own name.

Married people do not share a credit score, and you do not "inherit" your spouse's credit when you marry. You must have accounts with your own name on them in order to get points for your own credit score. They may be individual accounts or joint accounts.

If you are young and starting out, you can be an authorized user on a parent's account to help get established, but you must get credit in your own name alone ASAP! You want a minimum of three accounts to get approved to buy a home, and you only have to be 18 years old to become a home owner, so don't delay.

It takes six months from the time you open your first account to have a credit score. You need established credit for important things, such as qualifying to rent an apartment, financing an automobile, getting a discount on auto insurance, and buying a house or condominium.

2. Keep your accounts open.

You want to establish "old credit." Your age is not a factor in credit, but the age of your account is. You receive more points for longevity.

Closing a credit card could hurt your credit score, because it affects your debt-to-available-credit ratio. For example, if you owe a total credit card debt of $10,000 and your total credit is available is $20,000, you would be using 50% of your total available credit.

If you close a credit card with a $5,000 limit, you will reduce your available credit from $20,000 to $15,000; and change your ratio from 50% to 66%. This debt ratio increase will cause your score to go down.

3. Use your credit card at least twice a year to keep it active.

If you have a credit card you haven't used in years, you aren't receiving the good points from it that you could be. In fact, it could actually hurt you, because the credit card system thinks you might be getting ready to max out the card. But when you use the card for a minimal purchase two or three times a year, the system thinks you will not run up a sudden balance, because your history shows you use it minimally. Consequently, you receive more points to your score.

4. Pay off past credit cards that are *not charge-offs or collections.*

If you are late paying a bill, you want to get caught up immediately. On the other hand, if the account has already been transferred to collections or if it has become a charge-off, *do not* pay it off *if it is older than 24 months.* Why? Because old collections/charge-offs do not dock your credit score as severely, and if you suddenly pay on the old derogatory account, you will update the "Date of Last Activity" and cause your score to go down more! This isn't fair, but it is the way the system is set up, so we have to play the game accordingly.

Only pay off the old charge-off or collection *after* you get the agreement in writing that the creditor will remove it when they receive payment. (Verbal agreements don't count; get it in writing.)

5. Make sure your credit card company reports the maximum limit.

This is important, but it is something not a lot of people are aware of. If your credit card does not show what the limit is on your credit report (American Express is famous for this), then the scoring system assumes you are maxed out and lowers your credit score. *Ouch!* If you don't see the limit on your report, call the creditor and ask for it to be reported at once. If they say no, pay off the account to a zero balance and then store it securely, unused. That way, you will receive longevity points but won't be penalized for having a high balance-to-limit ratio. Don't be in a hurry to close the account. Let it set open with a zero balance.

6. Set up a system for paying bills on time.

You cannot change the past, but you can control what you do going forward. The credit system places the most emphasis on recent information. For example, a late payment one month ago docks more points than a late payment made a year ago. Therefore, time does gradually "heal" bad credit. Every month that passes helps, so be encouraged!

Pay your bills as soon as they arrive. There is no advantage to procrastination. If you don't have the funds to pay the entire bill as soon as it comes, that is an indication that you are living beyond your means. Therefore, you need to reduce spending and restructure your budget.

I recommend setting up automatic payment. That way, you don't have to worry about being late if a storm causes a delay in the mail delivery. If you tend to set aside bills or if you have ever lost a bill, then auto-pay is for you. Set it up today.

7. Use only one form of your name on all your credit accounts.

Established stability reduces confusion. With 300 million people in the U.S., there are likely to be other people with your name. If you use five forms of your name, you multiply your chances of being confused with another person. And if that person happens to have late payments, unpaid taxes, judgments, or liens, the last thing you want is to be mixed up with that person's credit.

8. Order a free copy of your credit report once a year.

Use this free report to check for accuracy and to guard against identity theft. The only place I recommend for getting your free report is www.annualcreditreport.com. It is the site authorized by federal law. I recommend getting the free report and not paying for credit scores, because the score you get are not the same scores the mortgage lenders get.

9. Pay your rent on time.

New laws are going to require landlords to report rent to the credit bureaus. This is good news! It has been frustrating for people who rent not to receive credit for their on-time rent payments, and I agree.

Rent is an important factor in determining how a person will pay their mortgage, so it should be included on the credit report. In the meantime, lenders always have and will continue to request a verification of your rent payment history from your landlord or property manager.

10. Make your mortgage your first priority.

Mortgage payment history is far more important than any other account when you go to refinance or buy another home. Don't make the mistake of taking turns paying your mortgage one month and your other bills the next month. Always protect the roof you sleep under and your precious home equity by paying your mortgage first, every month, and on time.

11. Do not take out a loan with a finance company.

Having a finance company on your credit report could lower your score, even if all the payments are made on time. This is because finance companies are considered to be hard money lenders. A hard money lender is a company that will lend to people who are hard up for cash or cannot qualify for a good loan elsewhere. Beware of furniture and window replacement companies that use a finance company. The same goes for financing a computer or other major item. Note: most automobile finance companies are not in this category; although, I can think of at least one hard money car seller that advertises on television that they finance anybody, regardless of credit.

Ask what company they set up financing with, and if it is a finance company, then you're better off setting up your own financing through your bank or credit union.

12. Do have two to three major credit cards.

A major credit card is one you can use anywhere, not only at a specific store. Visa, MasterCard, and Discover are major credit cards.

Having one credit card is insufficient. You want three trade lines to show on your credit report. Two could be credit cards and the third could be an auto loan, student loan, or an installment loan.

If you have three credit cards, there is no need to apply for more. Having too many credit cards will lower your score. Having more than six is just plain foolish, in my opinion. There is no need to have a whole pile of individual store cards, and too much credit hurts your score because of the potential debt.

If you already have more than three cards and those cards are more than three years old, keep them, because you are receiving points for longevity. You can still achieve a 800 score with more than three longstanding cards. Personally, I have five credit cards and my score is over 800. (All my balances are less than 10% of the limit, and I never carry a balance from one month to the next).

If you have ten or more cards, close a few of them that are the newest and least used. Ask that they be closed "by consumer's request" so it doesn't look like the creditor shut you down.

13. Pay down your credit card balances before paying extra on your auto or installment loans.

This strategy will give you a better score. What's more, the interest rate is usually higher on credit cards, so you don't want to carry a balance from month to month. It is a waste of your hard-earned money to pay interest, and it does not help your score to carry a balance. In fact, the opposite is true. If you pay your balance in full every month, you earn more points for doing so. To top it off, credit card interest is not tax-deductible, making it a ridiculous waste of money.

14. Keep your credit card balances below 30% of the limit at all times.

This is a very important strategy for gaining a A+ credit rating. If your balance-to-limit ratio is higher, points will be deducted, even if

142

all your payments are on time. And get this: if your balance-to-limit ratio is even one dollar over 50 percent, you will get even more points docked off your score. Thus, it is better to have several accounts with small balances than two accounts with high balances.

15. Refuse offers to open a new account in order to save 10% on your purchase.

Opening several new credit cards could lower your score by as much as *50 points*. So, don't fall prey to enticements from cashiers to open credit. The small upfront savings is not worth the hit to your credit score. I've seen people get denied for a home loan because they had too many store credit cards. You don't need a stack of individual store cards when you can use Visa or MasterCard pretty much everywhere.

16. Don't carry a lot of debt, even if you are wealthy and can afford it.

This is a mistake I often see on credit reports of dentists, physicians, and successful entrepreneurs. Remember, it is illegal to consider income in credit scoring; therefore, people with high incomes who can easily afford to carry a lot of debt are penalized on their scores if they carry a lot of debt, just as for people with modest incomes.

17. If you had a bankruptcy, check your credit for accuracy.

The vast majority of credit reports are incorrect for people who had a BK. Typically, accounts that were included in the BK still report as open. This hurts your credit, so follow-up as necessary to get those removed (or reported as closed if you are not trying to have the BK deleted).

18. If you had a bankruptcy, re-establish credit, but avoid debt.

After a BK, make sure you have some open, good credit. If all your accounts were discharged, you may need to apply for a couple secured credit cards to re-establish credit. But please resist the temptation to acquire new debt as an excuse for re-establishing your credit. This is not the time to take on an expensive auto loan that you don't need or cannot afford. To see a list of credit cards offered to people with damaged credit, go to http://www.creditcards.com/bad-credit.php.

19. If you are a shopaholic, take steps to break free.

Many people are obsessive-compulsive about shopping. They like to joke and call it "retail therapy," but it is no laughing matter. Eventually, debt grabs you by the throat and chokes all the fun out of your life. You end up working for your bills rather than for yourself—and that is no way to enjoy an abundant life!

The following are signs and symptoms of compulsive spending, as recognized by the Illinois Institute for Addiction Recovery:

- Shopping or spending money as a result of being disappointed, angry, or scared.

- Shopping/spending habits causing emotional distress or chaos in your life.

- Having arguments with others regarding shopping or spending habits.

- Feeling lost without credit cards.

- Buying items on credit that you would not buy with cash.

- Spending money gives you a rush of euphoria and anxiety at the same time.

- Spending or shopping feels like a reckless or forbidden act.

- You feel guilty, ashamed, embarrassed, or confused after shopping.

- Many of your purchases go unused.

- Lying to others about what you bought or how much money you spent.

- Thinking excessively about money.

- Spending a lot of time juggling accounts and bills to accommodate spending.

If some or all of these strike a chord, grab onto hope. Acknowledgement is the first step to recovery.

Practice self-talk daily—throughout the entire day —if need be. When you are tempted to soothe your stress or reward yourself by making a purchase, say to yourself, "I choose to be free from shopping addiction" and other positive statements that empower you to break free. Say no to using your credit card like cocaine. Invent other ways of filling the void. Write out your ideas and have the list handy. Here are some to get you started: go for a walk/run, call a friend, play tennis or other sport, listen to music, knit or crochet, garden, read an engrossing book, write in a journal, pray. If you have other good ideas, I'd love to hear them. (You can email me through my website.)

There are many inspirational books on breaking free of debt, such as those by Suze Orman, the respected financial advisor who was once a waitress deep in debt; as well as books by Mary Hunt, who pulled herself out of being $100,000 in debt. In addition, there is a good selection of self-help books available. Go to Amazon, Barnes & Noble, Christianbook.com, or other favorite bookseller and search "compulsive spending." Another option is to explore the self-hypnosis CDs on overcoming compulsive spending, also available from online booksellers.

If you would like to talk with a respected advisor, your local hospital may have a free service. If not, 1-800-522-3784 is a help-line that is open day and night.

Why not create a chart for getting out of debt, track your progress, and watch yourself get closer and closer to your goal? Get excited about changing your life. Others have done it, and you can do it, too!

The great apostle Peter wrote, "By what a man is overcome, to this he is enslaved."

If you have been enslaved by a shopping habit, you can break free!

CHAPTER 23

Is Credit Repair Ethical?

People have differing views about whether or not credit repair is ethical. It is not always as simple as yes or no. There are moral obligations, legal loopholes, and complexities to consider.

Indisputably, it is legal to declare "not guilty," to question an accuser/creditor, and to challenge the written proof. It is also legal for an accuser to drop the charges and for a creditor to "drop the late payment" off the record, or to give grace. Nevertheless, some people feel like getting a derogatory account deleted is unfair and dishonest. I would like to speak to that.

First, I agree with those who say lying is wrong. I do not advocate lying. Yes, some credit repair specialists and attorneys do lie for their clients. But others do not. I spoke with a credit repair specialist on the telephone recently who told me he will not work to get late payments or collections removed if they really happened. He only works to get errors, false information, and mistaken identity removed. His ethics and reputation are squeaky clean.

Other professional credit specialists are like defense attorneys in that they believe everyone has a right to a defense, even if they are guilty for one reason or another; therefore, they feel just fine about challenging the credit bureaus.

I promised, via the title, to reveal how professionals get negative items deleted, and I have done so. Now it is up to you to decide which strategies are appropriate for you. I do not make judgment calls for other people, nor do I decide where the gray area begins or ends for you.

Second, the credit scene is not as black and white as some people might think. There are many nuances and muddy waters in the field of credit. Following are two examples.

Family with the Sick Child

A certain married couple always paid every bill perfectly on time, and they both have A+ credit. Then out of the blue, disaster struck. Their dear child was diagnosed with leukemia. Like all good parents, they prioritized the life of their child above all else. The parents took their daughter to Children's Hospital in Seattle to be treated. Because they lived across the state, the mother and father rented a trailer and parked in the hospital parking lot as their temporary housing. As a Seattleite myself, I can see these trailers parked in the hospital lot when I drive past, and it is heartbreaking, knowing what they're there for.

These parents needed to be by their little girl's side while she fought for her life. Cancer treatment is expensive and treatments take months. Consequently, they let payments on other obligations slide. They went into debt. Their credit tanked.

When the medical disaster was over and the family was able to get back to their lives, how long should the parents be penalized? Should they be blocked from becoming home owners for the next seven years? Should they pay higher interest rates and insurance premiums—not because they are irresponsible deadbeats or careless, but because they had to use all their resources to save their child's life?

Or might it be appropriate that they take steps to clean up and restore their credit early?

The Woman with the Cheating Husband or the Man with the Cheating Wife

This scenario can go either way, and I've seen both. But the story I tell now was with a woman I met at a knitting group. She and her husband were married for many years. She loved him, worked as a homemaker, and raised their children. Then one day he told her he was moving on, that he had met a woman on a business trip to the Philippines, and that they were in love.

The wife learned her husband had used their credit cards to buy clothing and other items for his lover and for her family. In addition, he'd taken cash out of their joint account and had given it to the lover's family because they were, according to him, "more in need." Maybe they were in need, but that is beside the point. The point is betrayal.

The husband informed the wife he was filing for divorce and moving to the Philippines where he would then marry his new love. He did not plan on paying her any support, either.

He made good on his threat and did so. The wife was strapped with debt, because creditors "are not party to a divorce." Now that the husband was gone, the debt—the payment for all the lovely things purchased for the mistress and her family—now legally belonged to the woman who was now an ex-wife. The debt was such that she had to declare bankruptcy.

Her credit report showed a string of late payments plus a Chapter 7 BK. How long should this woman, who had her heart broken, be penalized financially as well? Would it be immoral for her to seek methods to get those derogatory accounts off of her report before seven long years?

I am not going to judge either of these two good citizens, because I have not walked their road. I am making the point that everyone's situation is different. All I can do is manage my own life and credit according to my own conscience. I hope others will do the same and not categorically condemn all credit repair. Personally, I leave the ethics and judging up to the individual and to God. I think that is fair, don't you?

CHAPTER 24

Conclusion

When you understand the credit system, you are empowered. You have the ability to create your own credit score by the choices you make. This, in turn, enables you to have better control over your finances and to obtain financing cheaper, quicker, and easier. You become a desired, sought-after client, which places you in the driver's seat for negotiating price.

Even more importantly, with excellent credit, you have a higher level of confidence and receive respect from others. You present a good witness for your faith and your family name to those you do business with.

Don't despair over past mistakes. The past is just that, the past— leave it there. The past does not define who you are. Accept grace and pardon. Move on with your life and create your own success story.

The future is yours to make as you will. The best is yet to come.

"For I know the plans I have for you," declares the Lord, "plans to prosper you and not to harm you, plans to give you hope and a future." ~ Jeremiah 29:11 NIV

How to Get the Letters in an Easy .Doc Format

Go to http://askcarolynwarren.com/credit-repair/. At the bottom of the page, use the contact form to ask for the letters. You will need to use the code: **Paid as Agred** to receive the letters to prove you purchased this book.

A Personal Note and How to Contact the Author

Thank you for purchasing this book. I wrote it to help good people improve their credit and financial situation in a manner that is effective.

If you found this book to be of value, I would greatly appreciate it if you would leave feedback on my Amazon book page, because feedback is essential for other readers.

In addition, if you have a quick question or comment, you are welcome to email me via my website, http://askcarolynwarren.com/. Click on "Ask Carolyn Warren a Question." I answer all messages.

I am state licensed in California and Washington for mortgage loans (NMLS # 1284134). I work for Envoy Mortgage, a full-service mortgage lender. If you are in California or Washington, please contact me about getting pre-approved. I know how to help people buy a home when they have less than perfect credit.

Made in the USA
San Bernardino, CA
14 November 2016